**PROFESSIONAL CONSTRUCTION MANAGEMENT
AND PROJECT ADMINISTRATION**
Second Edition

Architectural Record Books, New York, N.Y.
The American Institute of Architects, Washington, D.C.

PROFESSIONAL CONSTRUCTION MANAGEMENT AND PROJECT ADMINISTRATION

Second Edition

By William B. Foxhall
Senior Editor, Architectural Record

Published jointly by
**ARCHITECTURAL RECORD BOOKS AND
THE AMERICAN INSTITUTE OF ARCHITECTS**

The editors for this book were Hugh S. Donlan and Martin Filler.

The designer was Arthur Hawkins. Jacket design by Peter Bradford.

The production supervisor was Susanne LanFranchi.

The printer and binder were Halliday Lithographic Corporation.

Copyright © 1972, 1976 by Architectural Record
and The American Institute of Architects. All rights reserved.
Printed in the United States of America. No part of this
publication may be reproduced, stored in a retrieval system,
or transmitted, in any form or by any means, electronic,
mechanical, photocopying, recording, or otherwise, without
the prior written permission of the publisher.

Published by Architectural Record,
A McGraw-Hill Publication,
1221 Avenue of the Americas,
New York, New York 10020

and

The American Institute of Architects
1735 New York Avenue, N.W.
Washington, D.C. 20006

Library of Congress Cataloging in Publication Data

Foxhall, William B.
   Professional construction management and project
administration.

   Includes index.
   1. Construction industry—Management.　2. Industrial project management.　I. Title.
HD9715.A2F65　1976　　658'.99　　76-4483
ISBN 0-07-021755-6

PREFACE

The whole professional field of architecture and engineering has been helping me write this book for many years. For almost two decades of journalism in the mechanical engineering field and another one for *Architectural Record*, I have been granted literally hundreds of interviews by thoughtful and articulate practitioners. To all of these, my deepest thanks.

The converging forces of time and urgency that focus now upon the need for professional construction management as a definable set of ideas have been keenly perceived and eloquently described by a host of those practitioners. Robert F. Hastings crystalized many of those ideas in his writings and, as president of AIA, sparked the project of this book in January of this year. Acknowledgment is made of the guidance and review by the AIA task committee: S. Scott Ferebee, Jr., William Dudley Hunt, Jr. and Robert F. Hastings.

William B. Foxhall
September, 1971

SECOND EDITION

There has been a long and widely scattered search for a definition of professionalism in the practice of construction management. Some hold that if the practitioner works for a fee and avoids conflict of interest, he enters into the fold of the professional. There is a peril to architects and managers alike in believing—or even in suggesting—that working for a negotiated compensation rather than a profit tied to construction costs constitutes per se a professional service. That is a limited and destructive view. Professionalism lies not only in the mode of compensation but in: 1) the demanding education of the practitioner, 2) in his commitment to agency and service for his client, and 3) in a commitment to the public weal. Beyond all that, and perhaps primarily, the professional serves his own concept of a compelling human goal related to his personal talents.

Changes in construction management since September, 1971, have been by degree rather than substance. Field experience and the framing of contracts for construction management services have helped refine definitions and clarify professional relationships. AIA Document B801, Standard form of Agreement Between Owner and Construction Manager was issued in 1973 and followed by CM adaptations of other documents. The General Services Administration System for Construction Management was also updated and formalized in a revised edition dated April, 1975. Private practitioners have similarly outlined the scope and detail of their services. This edition reflects some of these and other developments.

W.B.F.—July, 1975

FOREWORD

Two words—*professional* and *management*—sound the keynote of response needed in today's near-crisis in building design and construction. Professionalism is the saving quality that preserves the fundamental and essential relationships between the client and those who design and deliver his building. Construction management is the operating instrument of professionalism in the whole process and, therefore, must itself be applied with professional integrity. It is the near-crisis, brought about by the accumulated, unresolved complexities and constraints of our time, that has called for this amplified role of management and the serious identity and support of professional roles. That is the reason for and intention of this book. No document, at this time, can offer the ultimate solution of all problems; but this review of both professional rationale and current practice is a step toward thoughtful progress in that direction.

Robert F. Hastings, FAIA
September, 1971

When Robert F. Hastings died in December, 1973, his writings and actions as chief executive of Smith Hinchman & Grylls had been monumental confirmation of his devotion to the highest order of professional integrity.

W.B.F.—July, 1975

And now another strong voice for excellence and quality and professionalism has been silenced. William Foxhall, editor of this book and editor of RECORD for many years, died on September 4, 1975.

Walter F. Wagner, Jr.—January, 1976

CONTENTS

1. The professional approach to management of the whole building process   1

    Sorting out professional lines   3
    New labels for sustained ideas   4
    Some arbitrary definitions   6

2. New ground rules for common sense   8

    Critical size and critical contractors   12
    Who's responsible for quality?   14
    When do interests conflict?   15
    Phased construction comes of age   16
    Who is responsible for construction?   16
    How to think about fees   19
    Where will management fees come from?   21

3. Organization for professional construction management   25

    Pre-construction management services   27
    CM services during construction   29
    Services of AE and project administrator   31
    Organization charts and forms   34

4. Anatomy of a project   36

    Steps in project analysis   38
    Budget control of the phased project   40
    Pursuit of the guaranteed max   43
    The management mix   46
    GSA studies the construction industry   46
    The World Trade Center   47
    Construction management Toronto style   49

A Boston campus poses every problem	52
Cost and management control	56
Four core concepts of CM	57
Management contracting at U. Cal.	58

5. Clients: public and private — 60

PBS procedures for selection and agreement	62
New York State: proving ground for principles	65
Upgrading New York's health facilities	68
Giant hospital tests N.Y. system	71
The private developer as client	74
What happens to quality	76
Management ability of developer is vital	77
Developer-manager-contractor arrangements	78

6. Contracts and proposals — 79

The prototype contract	83

7. Computers in perspective — 103

Components of the computerized system	106
Useful management reports	110
Role of the computer in cost control	119

8. Participating options of small professional firms — 121

1 THE PROFESSIONAL APPROACH TO MANAGEMENT OF THE WHOLE BUILDING PROCESS

Professionalism is an essential and inherent quality of every human process that combines both specially trained knowledge and dedicated action on behalf of a client. This is so because professionalism in both skill and integrity provides the only bulwark against failure or corruption of the process—be it judicial, medical, architectural or engineering. Further, the processes that must be served by the professions are the basic ones by which the human condition is uplifted and sustained.

When a creative art is one of the components of professional action—as it is in architecture—the whole process becomes servant to that art; and the requirement for professionalism extends all the way from the pre-design conditions fostering conception through the technical complexities of development and delivery of the finished building.

All of these ideas have had a long history of demonstration in classic client-architect-engineer-builder relationships. And in that portion of today's work that can be commissioned as to both scope and cost by one-man clients who can speak with a single responsible voice, the same ideas of professionalism are still clearly identified. But such clients are increasingly rare, even for projects of moderate scope. Instead, three compelling and confusing conditions have developed over the post-war decades until they have now reached near-crisis proportions in their combined power to obscure the enduring values of professionalism in our time.

First, the ever-larger works of man are now commissioned by the public client, the corporate client, the hospital board, the school board, the development consortium—a hydra-headed host of groups spending the money of other groups to whom they must report and be responsive. The consequences in make-shift checks and balances and in safe-action compromise have accumulated over the years like the waste products of evolution—to a point where only the muscle of professional management seems capable of cleaning the stables. There are, of course, the positive effects of united action, where again the sinews of management can pull great projects together.

But the elevation of "management" to the realms of magic has many dangers in it. Architectural abdication is paramount among those dangers. Let no architect believe that he is less than the constant and essential professional presence from start to finish of any project. Even the multi-client is entitled to that singular and able presence, that agency, unique in its guardianship of *every* aspect of their project's values. Then let no "manager" believe that he is more than instrumental to the practical support of that guardianship. Some of the modes of today's business may invite management to usurp the architect's agency where cost and speed are paramount. Individual architects themselves may shrink from the terrors of sheer technical complexity or the wounds of liability. But there is no escape from the classic one-to-one relationship of client and architect; and management is the means of its survival.

The second post-war condition that obscures professional identities is, again, one of proliferation in that the marshalling of professional and other skills for execution of large commissions entails the directed input of many individuals. That does not at all mean that only large architectural and engineering firms with an array of in-house specialists can enter into this complex arena. The multi-client and the multi-disciplined commission do indeed imply obvious burdens of clerical and communications tasks that, by themselves, would be beyond the scope of any one-man office. But the small-to-medium-sized office today is no stranger to consultation and joint venture. Those are but two of the many modes of marshalling expertise. Three not-so-new ideas or images need constant and confident redefinition in this context:

the image of the architect as leader in design phases, the contractor as responsible expert in construction phases, and the image of professional management as an instrument of efficiency throughout.

The third compelling condition that pervades all aspects of building design and construction today is inflation—under which the fixed budget (concomitant of the multi-client) wastes away in its purchasing power with every passing day. Management, again, is refining methods of contracting the time lapse from project start to completion. Phased or overlapped design and construction—for many years a familiar procedure in the pressured fields of industrial and urban commercial construction—is gaining more attention (and some new buzz words, like "fast track" and "UTAP") among other building types. Management methods for extending the scope and effectiveness of condensed schedules are being tested. The hazards and penalties of haste for its own sake are many and manifest; so, again, professionalism on the part of all team members—including managers—is the guardian of quality, as well as cost and time control.

SORTING OUT PROFESSIONAL LINES

Management itself is the skilled discipline of method and is not of and by itself professional within the context of our opening paragraphs. Neither, truth to tell, is architecture (—or engineering—or medicine—or law—) when its practitioners become entrapped in business without free and responsible agency toward their clients. That criterion of agency we now apply to the roles of management as they shift in emphasis from one phase of a project to another. The phases are not sequential like phases of the moon, but are concurrent, with interweaving surges of attention, like colored strands within a braid of common purpose.

Return now to ideas suggested at the beginning, wherein the processes are postulated servant to the art, and professions are set forth as ennobling to the state of man. Extend and adjust those notions to accommodate the natural limitations of individual practitioners. Consider the differences between comprehensive services and universal genius.

Then the architect of any of today's larger, multi-client works has the image of one man only in the singleness of his commitment and responsibility and in the consistent vocabulary of the building design. In actual performance of the work, the architect is a *firm* of organized and directed skills.

Similarly, the manager of one phase or another is a collation of skills and special knowledge; a firm of experts—not a super-being to be appointed as absolute dictator. He may, in fact, be an architect, or a consultant, or a contractor.

So, the conventional images evoked by the terms *architect, engineer, owner, contractor* and *manager* remain singular within the concept of fundamentally unchanging professional relationships; while in practice, each is many men and women who work for the common goal of services to clients—and to mankind, if you please.

When all these lines of image and endeavor are sorted out, we can discern three different management roles that bear upon and are mutually supportive of the fundamentally unchanged genesis and sequential logic of any architectural or engineering commission. One has identity with client decisions in matters of project need, feasibility, program, real estate, community relations and finance. We call him (or his firm) *project manager* or *project administrator*. The other two, under the generic label of *construction management*, have to do with the practique of design and delivery of the project itself within the client's budget. Both require detailed and current construction cost and method expertise, hence they are performed, in any practical situation, by a single firm acting as *construction manager*. It is important to keep in mind, however, that in the early phases of budget and design development, the input of construction management has to do with defining the cost-quality relationships of the architectural and engineering design options. As such, it could be more precisely labeled *construction consultation*. The second phase of construction management (which usually overlaps the first in time but not in function) is a control method for schedule and contract management—in short, *construction management* in its simplest connotations.

There are two good reasons for the triple separation described. The first is that each relates to a clear and separate focus in the role of professional agency toward the client. The second is that they all relate to the logic of the three-spoked wheel of Decision, Design and Delivery reproduced here from the article, "Proposal: a new and comprehensive system for design and delivery of buildings," by Robert F. Hastings in the November, 1968, issue of *Architectural Record*.

NEW LABELS FOR SUSTAINED IDEAS

The three segments of the 3-D wheel define the classic phases of attention that have always pertained to the generation of buildings: the decisions to build and to what purpose, scope and size; the design of the building; and the delivery (construction) of the building. Today, more than ever, those phases overlap, and the skills of delivery are germane—especially in large projects—to both the decision and design phases for reasons already outlined.

It is this condition of inter-permeation that brings us to grips now with the vital role of agency. The production skills of good contractors have long

THE PROFESSIONAL APPROACH TO MANAGEMENT

been—and continue to be—a reservoir of knowledge about technique and cost without which buildings simply cannot be built. Further, the costs to which each contractor commits himself have been—and continue to be—the real and final costs of each contractual component. Therefore, the successful contractor, as responsible entrepreneur, has conventionally had the ultimate responsibility for delivery of the building at a quoted price. For that he has been rightfully well-paid.

But two things have happened. First, the successful and responsible general contractor has withdrawn for good reason from both the competitive bidding of large work and the maintenance of diverse trade skills in his own work force. Second, the very skills and knowledge that have been his stock

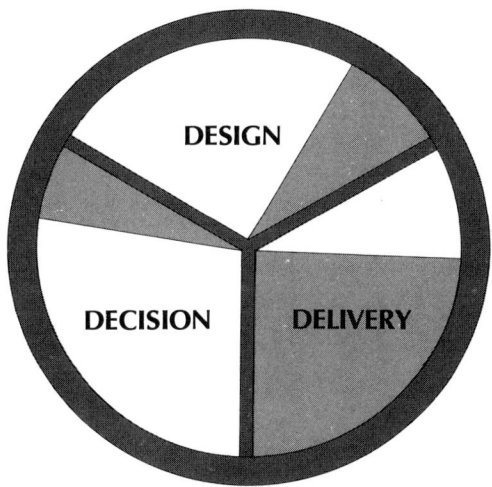

in trade are now needed to an increasing degree in the decision and design phases of building generation. But to purvey those skills in those phases, he must assume a role of professional agency toward the client just as the other professions do in those phases. He no longer works for a contractor's profit. He works for a professional fee.

Many contractors have found this transition difficult, but many have succeeded in it. In any case, the contractor's body of knowledge is neither mystic nor unique, and the capability for honest professional service in this field cannot be regarded as his exclusive domain. It is the professionalism of the service that is paramount, and staffing for its performance is key to its success.

So, may we not leave off anxiety and bickering and return to some admittedly arbitrary definitions of these professional services. Then, at least, we all can argue in one language.

THE PROFESSIONAL APPROACH TO MANAGEMENT

SOME ARBITRARY DEFINITIONS

What is a *project manager* or (some prefer) *project administrator*? He is the client's voice, agent and purse string. He rings the starting bell when a project exists as serious intent. He makes or expedites the owner's decisions at key points as the project develops. He may be one man or a department on staff of a sophisticated client. He may be a consultant firm or a developer. He may be, in fact, a special kind of architect. He is the rim and the spokes of our project wheel. He may or may not have detailed, technical construction expertise among his own resources. If he has, he should ideally use that knowledge only for communication with and critique of the building design and delivery processes. If he is tempted to use it for direct input or control of those processes, he should recognize that a fundamental shift in his role is implicated and that there is a possible conflict of interest in that change. For example, as project administrator, he may be called upon for an ownership decision regarding a change that he himself has proposed while acting in the role of construction manager. The conflict is admittedly more philosophical than dangerous in most cases, but should be recognized as a real possibility.

What is a *construction manager*? "He" is a *firm* that applies knowledge of construction techniques, conditions and costs to the three phases of decision, design and delivery of a project. First, as *construction consultant* he clarifies the time and cost consequences of decision and design options as they occur. Second, as *construction manager* he enters, still as a professional, into construction scheduling, prepurchasing of critical materials, advising on the method of obtaining contractors and awarding contracts, and coordination and direction of all construction activities, including those of the producers of systems and sub-systems.

Some will recognize the last few phrases as echoing a definition developed during a December 1970 workshop of DHEW/FECA in which representatives of every sector of construction, public and private, participated. Further details of definition, derived from similar researches of GSA, will be developed later.

This concern of public agencies with thoughtful analysis of current crises in construction will undoubtedly determine ultimate language usages in this field—at least insofar as *project management* and *construction management* are concerned. It is not only their giant purchasing power that prevails in this matter. It is also their clear acknowledgment of the primary role of professional agency in the management of public works and publicly supported construction that is being stated in terms of common usage. However limited in inherent clarity those usages may be, they will probably establish the ultimate connotation for these terms.

THE PROFESSIONAL APPROACH TO MANAGEMENT

Now it is time to call another spade a spade. The reason for this proper searching of the soul in public method is the virtual breakdown in effectiveness of the status quo. The laudable intent of legislation requiring acceptance of the low bid out of a public invitation simply has not been realized. Nor has the similar intent of legislation calling for multiple sub-section contracts. All of this is for later discussion, but the fact is: *Someone* has to be responsible for *quality,* cost and time control, and the low-bid, multi-contract method simply has not worked as a guardian of quality—nor even of time and cost, when all changes are counted. So we now call for *professional* management to do two things: First, to enlist competent skills that have been by-passed under the non-qualified, low-bidder system; second, to apply those skills early enough to sustain quality and value within the budget during design development—rather than to accept those post-bid cuts that never seem to save as much as their itemized bid cost and certainly do less for overall quality than an equivalent saving effected as a design alternate before bidding takes place.

Architect George T. Heery, whose firm, Heery & Heery, has developed successful methods of applying construction management to his own and other architects' projects, has written a succinct definition in his book, *Time, Cost and Architecture* (McGraw-Hill, 1975):

"Construction management is that group of management activities, over and above normal architectural and engineering services, related to a construction program—carried out during the predesign, design, and construction phases—that contributes to the control of time and cost in the construction of a new facility."

2 | NEW GROUND RULES FOR COMMON SENSE

"It's really all just common sense."

That is the consensus of almost every conversation, report, interview and publication so far on the subjects of project management, project administration, construction management and construction consultation as those terms are taking on new meanings in the language of building design and construction.

In so huge and fragmented an industry facing the dual crises of inflation and technological change, no wonder there are fears and charges, self-serving thrusts and counter-charges on every side.

But as those terms gain definition, what had appeared to some as a threat of invading special interests against familiar professional and trade practices is revealed as simply a new array of method for accomplishing the ancient purposes of design and construction under new conditions.

Method, here, means management: no more—and no less—than the

NEW GROUND RULES FOR COMMON SENSE

skilled application of sophisticated tools for the accomplishment of complex purposes. And in the special context of building design and construction, method means management on a professional level, of all professional services as well as of all the commerce and complexity of modern building. It is in the realms of commerce and complexity that management prevails.

There are no new professions.

There are a few new roles and relationships; a few dramatic shifts in project scale; many and complex changes in the profiles of project ownership. We have outlined in Chapter 1 the three basic areas of agency relating to the management function. In somewhat more detail, they are:

Project management or project administration comprises those skills that must be brought to bear by or on behalf of the client when a need for new or expanded facilities is recognized, analyzed, programed, evaluated and budgeted. The project administrator then:

1) relates value to probable cost,
2) seeks and evaluates real estate,
3) sets up funding arrangements,
4) participates in detailed programing,
5) relates current program to future needs,
6) lists professional (including management) skills required,
7) relates those skills to client's in-house capacities,
8) participates in seeking and commissioning professional skills.

The post-commitment role of the project administrator is to: 1) assess the performance of nominated professionals in relation to the program, 2) maintain cash flow, 3) ride herd on the project in general, not intruding into the skills of design or construction, but providing management support and authority by which design and construction professionals can be effective.

Construction management has been described as developing in two phases. The first, *consultation* during design development, provides cost and construction method information relative to objectives of the budget. The second is post-bid *management* by which the various contractual components of the project are assembled, sequenced and related to the cash flow. Both of these functions are implied by the generic term, "construction management," since both are performed by the same firm.

There is a variation of these definitions that combines construction consultation and construction management together with feasibility studies, programing and other services, labeling the whole process as "project management." This definition can be sustained in a semantic sense, but only up to the point where the roles of agency are clearly defined. At that point, the image of the client and his project administrator as inciting force and ownership presence in the project, and the separate images of the architect and construction manager as effectuating forces, must be maintained lest the confusion of their roles further obscure the issues that are before us.

In simplest terms, then, the project administrator is effectively the client's voice, or at least the nearest approach today's multi-client can make to one-voice response to the project requirements. The construction manager is a firm capable of early and *professional* application of resources of general construction cost and method knowledge as it affects the design stipulations of the professional architect and engineer. Today's inflexible budgets now impose upon both architect and construction manager a requirement for rapprochement of their several skills toward the successful completion of the job.

Among honest men of good will, it makes no real difference to integrity of their professional roles whether the contractual agency of the construction manager is toward the owner or toward the architect. Any architect's fears, that parallel agency of the manager interposes an onerous spoiler or wielder of a ruthless and insensitive paring knife between himself and the project, presuppose a non-professional (or worse) body in the manager's role. Such fears, in fact, belittle the very concept of professionalism, in which the architect's own stake is obvious. Similarly, any manager's view of the architect as an extravagant artist (at best) denies a long and documented history of competence and impugns the manager's own competence for judgment on the professional level. The manager cannot design or specify. Only the architect can. Nor can the manager enforce any design or specification recommendation in which both architect and owner (project administrator) do not concur.

Today, there is a trend toward the breaking up of large jobs into multiple contracts. The force behind this trend is the simple fact that single general contractors have been responding less and less to public invitations to bid on large work. The bidding process itself became inordinately expensive, and as more and more general contractors divested themselves of trade work forces, their bidding input became the result of assembling the bids of subcontractors. Further, the pleas of organized subcontractors to be relieved of the expense of responding to the requests of several general contractors for estimates on single jobs (for which they may or may not have had a real probability of access by competitive bid) were instrumental in the passage of several state laws requiring multiple contracts to some degree. Meanwhile, large successful general contractors turned more and more to negotiated contracts in one form or another—which automatically excluded them from public works.

Thus, the emergence of the multiple contract form of construction has had a three-fold drive. First, the already cited response of legislative bodies at every level from municipal to federal to the manifest depletion of available skills under the single contract system was to enact regulations requiring that contracts for public work be let on the multiple contract basis. In part, this was to get around probable constitutional inhibitions against restricted listing and invitation of pre-qualified general contractors. In part, it was the increasing reluctance of general contractors to bid at all. Mainly, however, the hope was to reach deeper into the reservoirs of knowledge represented by the daily work of subcontractors and to spread the base of responsible activity in public work. When management of the over-all project became an obvious problem (especially as the urgencies of phased construction became paramount), many legislative bodies stipulated that the over-all management should be the responsibility of one of these multiple prime contractors, usually the one in the civil or general construction field of activity. It soon became evident that this responsibility added to the activities of one contractor would be inoperable unless some way was found to augment the basic fees of that particular contractor. Even then, the input was limited to the post-bid phase and was further limited by capabilities and motivation of the assigned contractor. It just didn't work well, and this may have been the real generating motive of the construction management idea as now defined. That idea gained the additional theoretical advantages of re-enlisting the skills of qualified large contractors on a professional rather than a publicly competitive basis, and extending their effectiveness back into the decision and design phases of project development.

The second drive toward the multiple contract resides in the inflationary spiral. As time itself became more and more critical as a cost factor in performance of the contract, phased or overlapped construction during design development became increasingly the way of life in all kinds of projects over a practical minimum cost of, say, $3 million. An HEW study reports possible savings of 8 to 12 per cent in dollars; and the "Fast-Track" study prepared by Caudill Rowlett Scott for the New York State University Construction Fund proposes possible savings of 25 to 45 per cent in time. The experience of Smith, Hinchman & Grylls on phased SUNY projects bears out these projections. (See Chapter 4, page 36.)

The third force behind the practice of the multiple contract was the urgent need to take advantage of local capabilities in the performance of any project contract. In order to do this, it became necessary to enlist the local talent at a level of capability represented by the subcontracting fraternity. Hence, the subcontractors were increasingly invited to bid as primes on work in their area. Where the bonding of contractors for public work was a requirement, this had the additional advantage of spreading the over-all bonding into more moderate packages—an idea that seems to be gaining favor among bonding carriers.

There has been, therefore, a combination of circumstances, both public and private, forcing the industry toward the multiple contract form of bidding, while at the same time, the vacuum created by absence of the profit-motivated general contractor with his coordinating skills, as well as his delivered-price commitment, is being filled by a host of eager firms who may or may not realize the dimensions of the task they so willingly undertake.

It is important for architects to recognize at this point that the handling of multiple contract forms of bidding and letting the over-all project is not a simple extension of the comprehensive services idea. That idea simply extends the concept of agency over a broader base of representation toward the client. Multiple-contract procedures, on the other hand, introduce a whole new set of agency roles which architects must be prepared either to provide themselves or to share with other competent professionals. Further, the system imposes a whole new set of management requirements for which architects must be prepared to either staff themselves or enlist the aid of those who are already prepared to handle these matters. The roster of firms so prepared is not a long one, but it is one studded with a few architectural and engineering firms who have learned the business of construction contract management over difficult years of practice and growth. Other competent firms have evolved from the general contracting sector of the industry. Some have grown up from the specialties of cost consultation. Some have evolved from the field of general management consultation. Whatever their genetic threads may be, there are two overriding essential qualities of successful firms in this field: 1) They must have currency in their access to field-tested cost data and construction method over wide geographic distribution. 2) They must be professional in their offerings of service to clients.

CRITICAL SIZE AND CRITICAL CONTRACTORS
Many general contractors have voiced apprehension and opposition to the dual ideas of phased construction and construction management on the logical grounds that phased construction means multiple contracts, and that construction management, as recommended for phased projects, means an end to the conventional role (hence, presumably, the livelihood) of general contractors on such "piecemeal" projects. As the method spreads, they see an end to the general contractor and to the cost reductions and delivery advantages they claim are inherent in the single contract method. More especially, they and others of their less apprehensive colleagues vocally mourn the loss of the "fiscal responsibility" represented by the lump-sum commitment of the general contractor's single bid.

This impeccable logic is unhappily, albeit understandably, based on three major misapprehensions.

First, phased construction is not new, not proposed as a magic panacea, and not a threat to contractors, general or otherwise.

Second, construction management is not new except in expansion of its professional application, is not proposed as a magic panacea, and is, in fact, an opportunity for general contractors.

Third, "fiscal responsibility" comes into better perspective when one begins to search for those general contractors who can actually make a responsible lump-sum single bid that will *really save the client money* on a $10-million, $100-million, $300-million or $500-million project. Work on this scale is far from rare today, but the universe of available bidders shrinks so rapidly as the scale increases that competition virtually disappears early in the lower half of such a scale; and in the upper half, even the brave and the rich contractors measure their responsibility and risk in such terms of honest profit that the client's "savings" through single-contract efficiencies are, to say the least, difficult to measure.

When any of the current forms of negotiated construction contract (cost-plus-percentage, cost plus fixed fee, guaranteed maximum, etc.) is used, the control and management procedures of the construction phase are very similar to those applied under the "construction management" system as now defined—with three important differences. Under a typical negotiated contract, the contractor's management controls:

1) are applied as a business for profit—not as a professional service for the client;

2) make no contribution to design development—except as they are commissioned to advise on costs etc. on a fee basis;

3) are applied without the itemized scope and content of most CM contracts, hence may focus more on the contractor's than the owner's behalf.

So there is a critical dollar size and degree of complexity above which the professional construction management of multiple-contract, phased construction projects becomes the logical, if not the only feasible method of project design and delivery. Similarly, below that critical point, the cost of performing all the construction management services professionally exceeds the practical returns of other more conventional methods.

That is so because the minimum investment in the tools of the trade and in personnel required for the honest proffering of professional management services above the critical cost point represents a standby force that would result in extravagant over-kill if applied below that critical point. Even if the manager's fee (viewed as a per cent of construction cost) is increased inordinately on the low side of the critical point, the effectiveness of sophisticated method soon drops below that of simpler conventional methods insofar as either savings or efficiency is concerned.

NEW GROUND RULES FOR COMMON SENSE

The exact dollar amount of the critical point is, so far, indeterminate from either the client's or the professional's point of view. First, because it is a function of complexity and location as well as of absolute cost. Second, because its value to the client varies with the cost of his money and the value of a crash program toward soonest occupancy. Third, because its management goal is to implement architectural solutions to total client needs, which include a varying premium on quality. Highest quality does not *necessarily* mean protracted time. Dollar for dollar, however, it does mean a shift in emphasis during the design development phase that calls for genuine professional orientation of the construction manager as consultant during that phase.

WHO'S RESPONSIBLE FOR QUALITY?
The subject of quality brings up another of the protestations of certain contractors to the effect that the single contract at the lowest bid assures required quality at the lowest price, since quality is established by the bidding documents to which competing contractors must all respond. Logic, again. But as the general contractor turns more and more to the brokerage of subcontracts and the management thereof, he relies for much of the cost input to his own bid on the quotations he receives from a pool of subcontractors. If he subcontracts, say, 80 to 85 per cent of the work, and he shares the subcontractor pool and its quotations with other general contractors bidding on the same job, he is left with only two variables within which to meet his low bid: the cost of his own small portion of the work and the cost of his management. Since he is not likely to do his own share of the work for nothing, his alternative is to cut his management.

The fallacy that quality resides in the documents is equally germane, since quality depends a good deal also on performance qualifications and experience of the contractor. The broker who is low bidder is not selected on the basis of qualifications but only on price. If his low price is preamble to limited management and a profit on change orders, he does damage to himself and his profession as well as to the project, the architect and the owner.

Architects have not yet found a way to specify levels of management by contractors in their bidding documents as they do levels of quality in materials. The separate contracting for professional construction management in the post-bid phase seems to be one way to approach this problem, since the items of management activity can be fairly well defined in the contract. Many general contractors have found ways to provide this service for a professional fee, and when they thus become true agents of the owner, their skills are unsurpassed in this phase. This does not mean that contractors' advices during design development are automatically superior. Conceptual costing and value analysis of design alternatives call for an entirely different set of historical and regional cost knowledge and a much more sophisticated approach to both ownership and design objectives than are inherent to the general contractor's accustomed role. Again, this does not mean that contractors are automatically hampered in or precluded from this area of professional advice. It means, quite simply, that first-cost pricing is not the sole criterion of the value of design alternatives, and further that the contribution of professional construction management to design development is on so broad a base of information and technique that any practitioner, contractor or otherwise, needs special resources.

WHEN DO INTERESTS CONFLICT?

In the matter of the contractor's capability for professional performance, it is apparent that considerable re-orientation of his usual role must be developed. For example, the general contractor is normally committed to a role of advocacy for the subcontractor in his dealings with the owner. In any dispute or evaluation regarding changes, for example, the contractor normally adjudicates the proposals and billings of the subcontractor. Even if he finds it necessary (or expedient) to revise the subcontractor's hopes downward to an acceptable agreement, when he then transmits that to the owner, he is acting on behalf of the subcontractor. If he were a construction manager, he would have a reversal of role at this point and would be under professional obligation to evaluate all proposals entirely from the owner's point of view. Further, he would have to gain the support of the architects as well as the owners in order to make these proposals effective.

If a construction manager is selected from among the general contracting sector of the industry, and the contractor selected happens to have other work current in the region, for which he is acting as general contractor, it is an inherent conflict of interest in any situation where (a) the contractor's own personnel may be divided in their attentions between the two (i.e., the management and the contracting) jobs and (b) he has to deal with one or more subcontractors who are working on both jobs. If, for example, subcontractor X is essential to the success of Job A and is also in some sort of dispute on Job B (for which the same general contractor is construction manager) it would be expecting too much to suppose that the general contractor as construction manager would represent the owner without conflict in disciplining subcontractor X on Job B to the point where he might become ineffective on Job A.

Many public construction agencies and some large corporate clients who regularly commission construction management services have taken cognizance of these possible conflicts of interest by stipulating full-time assignment of key personnel of the construction management firm to their projects—whether or not the management firm is also a general contractor.

PHASED CONSTRUCTION COMES OF AGE

Many architects—several, anyway—react to the terms "phased construction" and "fast track" as though they were observing children re-inventing the wheel. These architects tend to be in fairly large firms which have developed over the years through services to the industrial sector of the client universe. They point out that phased construction has been a way of life in that sector for many many years. Their own professional practices have developed competent and highly sophisticated procedures for accommodating to that way of life. They further report no conflict with the contracting fraternity in making these methods effective. They inquire blandly: "So what's new?"

Well, application of the method to several billion dollars worth of educational buildings is new. And to hospitals and medical centers. And to vast public works. All these are new to the method; and the entrance of a whole new universe of clients including the public, as already described, has introduced complexities to application of the method and requirements for its management vastly different from those which have been so successfully applied to the austere, single-slab rectangles of industry.

That is not to imply that the architects for industry have been insensitive or laggard in their development of these methods for application to an increasing diversity of building types in their own practices. Indeed, the evolution of those methods owes much of its success to the inventive diligence of those architects and the proving grounds of that burgeoning diversity.

In any case, the passage of time, the increase of technical complexity, the tightening of economic imperatives, the search for methods to preserve human values of the client-architect-builder continuity in a world where all three may have become large corporations or public agencies, all these comprise a new construction milieu in which specialized management and expertise—with phased construction where it makes sense—are earning an essential role with its own just compensation.

WHO IS RESPONSIBLE FOR CONSTRUCTION?

The ultimate responsibility for all construction lies with the owner. It is the owner's participation in every aspect of his project that ultimately accounts for its success or failure. Capability for that participation has been lacking in the past, but under the conditions of today's economy, the multi-client can no longer afford to remain aloof and rely on packages of documents and conventional contracting practices to deliver an acceptable building. The stringencies of budget alone require a continuing ownership presence (project administrator) to make decisions as options of design and delivery occur.

In a series of talks about the crisis in construction, Gerald McKee, Jr., president of McKee-Berger-Mansueto Inc., has pointed out that the internal frictions and external pressures that have brought the industry to current needs for phased construction and construction management are neither inflation nor the premise that labor is unbridled in its power. The crisis in labor, he says, is only a symptom of the fact that the industry has been so rigidly structured that it has not been able to change of its own volition, despite the fact that it is treated as though it were an example of classic 19th century economics wherein supply and demand would automatically generate changes for viability. But, even granting the power of supply and demand, it can't operate because of the in-grown restrictions of the industry and the bodies of public law and code (as well as in-grown documentary and bidding processes) that virtually eliminate the ability to respond as other industries do.

One of the practices of the past, that still has traces remaining today, is the attitude on the part of owners and architects that the solution of a building design problem can be expressed in a set of perfect documents that can transmit all the owner's wishes to a general contractor. The notion persists that the contractor can then set to work and deliver the building. Today's conditions increasingly demonstrate the fact that this cannot be done. Yet most of the disputes that arise in projects today arise from the fact that people continue to believe that it can be done. The situation is common wherein a contractor may reach a point of confusion at which he protests that he cannot proceed without clarification. The owner calls upon the architect to tell him how to proceed. The architect replies that instructions for procedure are in the documents. The contractor replies that instructions are not sufficiently clear. He is well aware that a procedural directive at this point has implications of liability. The consequence is that there is an artificial arresting of all development at the bidding-document stage, based on an assumption that the contractor should need nothing more and the design process is finished except for observation of its execution.

This set of attitudes, says McKee, not only does not work because of its intrinsic unreality (purposely overstated here), but it forces delay of commencement of the work until the mythical perfect bidding documents have been prepared. This almost automatically costs 30 to 50 per cent more in time than more rational approaches are now demonstrating to be necessary.

Today's practice increasingly reinforces the realization that the ultimate responsibility for construction really rests with the owner. That was also the case in the past, but the means of implementing the owner's participation were not part of conventional practice so that private owners especially were unable to participate to an effective degree. Now owners, faced with the consequences of delay, are insisting that, since the responsibility is theirs, the risks, and therefore also the profits of participation must also be theirs.

Where the owner's sophistication in matters of construction is limited, the consultant *project administrator* (whether his professional identity be architect, contractor or otherwise) finds a role in implementing the owner's insistence on participation. Not only do owners gain in the upgraded performance of all concerned by accepting the risks involved, but they also are relieved of the untenable position of trying to lay all of the risks and their consequences on the architect and the contractor.

What are some of the things that a project administrator who is truly the agent of the owner can do that the architect would be either unable to do or would find excessively onerous? Mr. McKee cites the case where a contractor reported that a certain material in the specifications was directed to be applied in accordance with the manufacturer's recommendations. The manufacturer refused to offer recommendations in the particular situation at hand. The contractor then asked for further instructions. The architect has investigated various modes of applying the material and believes he has a solution. He says to the project administrator: "We think we know what to do and what is the best way of applying this material, but if we tell the contractor what to do, not only is he not responsible if it fails, but we acquire a substantial liability. We believe the responsibility for the decision here should rest with the owner."

The project administrator, as owner's agent, advises the owner that if he does not make the decision here, the consequent delays will be substantially more costly than the actual failure of the material. So the project administrator advises the owner to instruct the contractor to proceed.

In practice, architects are beginning to welcome this kind of intercession in relief of their own liability position which has become increasingly burdensome. But there is considerable apprehension among individual architects that the process involves some central loss of their professional image. This is particularly true among individual architects or small architectural offices whose commissions are only occasionally in the cost scale where construction management would be applicable. To that numerically large group, the notion of a new profession called "construction management" seems disturbing until the actual lines of professional protocol are more clearly understood. Many articles in the popular press and even in some quasi-architectural publications have fed those fears with images of talent overshadowed by management. As a matter of strict fact, architects have been the purchasers of management in support of their basic talents for many years—either through staff appointments or through consulting services. Many architects, especially the smaller ones, would willingly expand the consultation roster in cost control and management areas substantially if they could find a way to accommodate such consultation within the normal fee structure. On small jobs, of course, small-to-medium-sized architectural firms who are adequately staffed can and do perform many of the services now being defined as project administration and construction management. In smaller work, these services are often absorbed into standard fees.

As the canons of professional project administration and construction management become more thoroughly defined, and the scale of project to which they apply is more widely and readily identified, the conditions in the industry may very well provide acceptable expectations of fee for those services similar to the acceptance of the existence of (not necessarily adequacy of) fees of engineers and other supportive professionals. Problems in the establishment of such acceptances are being solved with repeated demonstrations of the fact that the time and cost advantages of this kind of management are compensation in themselves. Some small- and medium-sized architectural firms today are looking into the possibility of permanent arrangements with consulting and/or contracting firms whereby they can offer clients ready access to these management skills and savings.

HOW TO THINK ABOUT COMPENSATION[1]

From the construction management firm's point of view, there is also a rather high minimum project construction cost below which the assembly of services that can be offered in good conscience within the limits of fees available today becomes either uneconomical or non-professional. Services, of course, run the whole gamut from the simplest cost consultation to full scale, sophisticated, computerized control methods complete with full-time staff both for management and communication and for field inspection and job coordination. The full roster of such services will be shown in later chapters. The point here is simply that the client will get whatever services he pays for, and the fee for construction management services will have to be on a sliding scale with relation to job cost just as it is in other professional fees. It should be noted that the percentage scale is only a guide to a fixed fee that should not vary with actual delivered costs at the given project scope. Compensation should actually be calculated on a basis of manhours required.

For example, for a $2.5 million project, the construction management fee might be on the order of 2 per cent for the simplest cost consultation during design development, general construction advice throughout the project and periodic scheduling services during the delivery phase. If the

---
[1] The word "fee" in this text should be read as "compensation" for strict conformity with emerging AIA usage.

job is to be run on a phased construction multi-contract basis, so that a full-time field representative will be necessary, that 2 per cent fee might well be doubled. A full-time field representative is a fixed cost to the job, and in the $2.5 million range, such a fixed cost looms much larger as a per cent than would the services of the same representative on a much larger job.

Consider the fact that the fixed costs in staffing up and processing the management for a $5 million project are about the same as those for a $10 million project. The intermittent servicing by resources of the firm would of course differ from one job to the other. But, while the need for a sliding scale of fees is an obvious result of these conditions, those fees must be developed and negotiated on a basis of manhour calculations for stipulated services. They are only indirectly related to project cost.

To date, there has been no industry-wide standardization either of construction management fees or of the services a given fee might represent. Some indicators are developing, especially as government agencies develop experience in these matters. For example, both GSA and the New York State Facilities Development Corporation have set a minimum of $5 million as the project budget for which construction consultation professionals are to be commissioned. The New York agency has established a one per cent fee for construction management services on all projects above that $5 million critical point. They provide, however, for certain compensated expenses such as the salaries (minus fringe benefits) of a stipulated number and identity of personnel assigned on a full-time basis to the project by the construction manager. These reimbursed expenses are intended to accommodate the construction manager's fee to the scope of the work. The managing firm also separately contracts to take care of general requirements (field office, access, security, etc.) on the job site.

Incidentally, this New York agency, which has pioneered in applications of the construction management principle, recruits construction managers solely from the general contractor sector of the construction industry. They have been able to develop, through rigorous insistence, the professional responsibilities of the manager's input to design development phases of the work. Their method is to propose at least three qualified construction management firms from which the architect of the project selects his preference as a professional with whom to work. Many architects report that these arrangements have been satisfactory, and indeed salutary, to development and delivery of their projects.

In summary, then, there appears to be a critical project size on the order of about $5 million for which some certain package of construction management services seems appropriate. Some consultants point out that the roster of services can be trimmed to lesser budgets provided that professional integrity is maintained and the client is advised of the scope of services he is getting. At least one construction management consultant firm has established a $15 million project cost as a minimum for which they will offer full management services. Other firms have stipulated minimum packages of services below which they cannot work effectively and professionally. In any case, neither contractors nor other professionals, including architects, appear to have much cause for apprehension about loss of power or control so long as the integrity and value of their professional services and agency toward clients is maintained.

WHERE WILL MANAGEMENT FEES COME FROM?
Many owners and architects have supposed that the fees for professional construction management will be the "price" of filling the management voids of absent general contractors. But there is more to it than that. There is, of course, the simplistic response that, in conventional projects, the cost of management (however ill-defined in scope) is already present in the contractor's bid. In addition to the fact that this is an illusive amount virtually impossible to translate into any rational fee structure, there is also the fact that it is related to outmoded conditions in the construction industry.

The increasingly active participation of large, sophisticated clients is accelerating the search for new methods. In addition to phased construction and construction management, there are the emerging potentials of industrialized or systems building, turnkey, component pre-bidding, life-cycle costing and many other factors that can profoundly affect the structure of the whole design and construction process. These clients, public and private, wish to maintain their own flexibility of option throughout the process. Further, they want to know what professional parts architects, engineers, contractors and consultants are ready, able and likely to play in the process—and how they are to be paid for their roles.

The client's need for flexibility in the exercise of options (as to, say, multiple or package contracting, with professional construction management) supports the logic of a time-basis professional fee structure, but meets a serious constraint on large projects for either corporate or public clients in that many of these cannot enter into open-ended agreements for professional services. Both scope of services and upset dollar value of fees, with pre-established bases and limits for added charges, must be spelled out in their agreement.

Well, even the biggest multi-client can't expect to have it both ways—both flexible options and fixed fees. Even the conventional design-bid-build process has built-in provisions for: extra services, reimbursable costs, contingencies, change orders, etc. These, too, have had to meet strict budget limits. The only real urgency for option-flexibility is for the saving of time and/or money within the design quality standards. Any substantial change in scope of project program has always been subject to renegotiation.

So, under today's changing conditions, many client and professional groups are considering the following:

1) A *movable* upset amount budgeted for professional compensation for design and/or management;
2) The initial upset to be established as a lump sum plus specific reimbursable costs for clearly defined basic services to the whole project which is also defined as to both scope and target duration;
3) A set of defined increments of service representing certain procedural options (such as an increase in number of contracts, field personnel, etc.);
4) A means of predicting compensation for those options,
   a. As time-based proposals from the professionals involved,
   b. As a negotiated increase of basic professional compensation on any rational basis;
5) A contingency reserve for fee increments and reimbursables as options are taken;
6) That reserve to have some flexibility based on the rationale of budget savings accruing to each option;
7) A roster of reimbursable expenses including certain field personnel and added insurance protection as management or scheduling of the work of others entails increased staff and risk.

It would be naive to suppose that every act or service of every professional could be assigned a dollar value for entry into any of the above calculations. The list of construction management services alone (see Chapter 3) bears this out, and, of course, every architect and consulting engineer has known it all along.

Nevertheless, there are three basic and familiar resources for setting up and funding time-based professional fees. 1) Fees for one package called "planning, design and documentation" (AE fees!) have been subject to negotiation calculated on a time-plus basis for many years. 2) Post-bid management services have been paid for conventionally out of general contractors' margins covering management, profit and risks. While man-hour records of the management portion of those margins are not consistently reported or available, some averaging of margins might be derived for at least a ballpark target upset for these services. 3) Construction costs themselves are matters of record as are the effects of escalation, so that the quoted fees of those who propose to shorten construction time or otherwise lower costs through professional services can be evaluated.

NEW GROUND RULES FOR COMMON SENSE

The accompanying chart visualizes some of these notions. It is adapted from one prepared by Donald J. Stephens of the Albany, N.Y. region, based on ideas expressed through the many AIA committees, state and national, in which he is active.

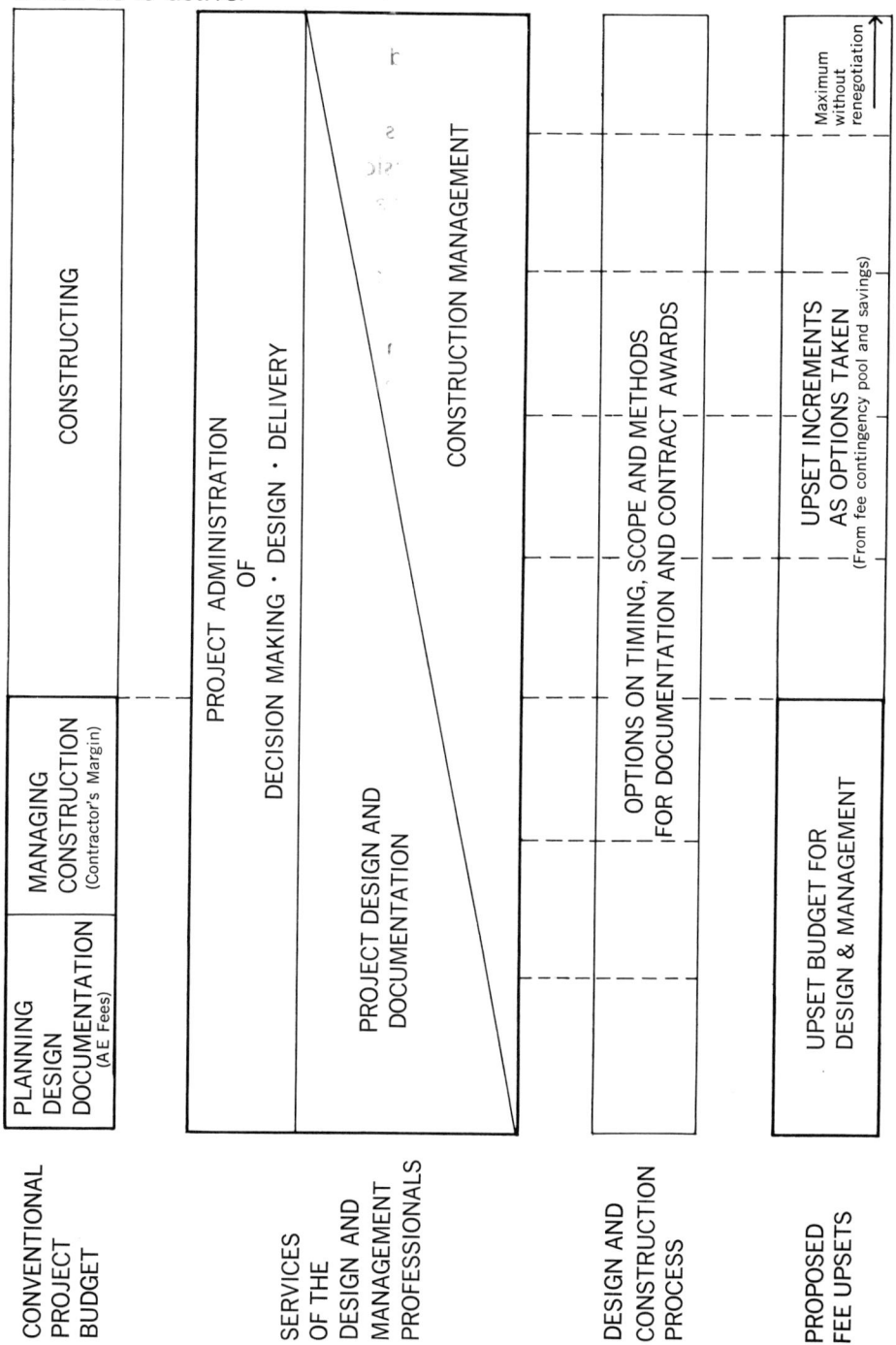

There is no doubt that much data-gathering and analysis (not to say legislative action) will precede ultimate solutions of all fee problems. Already, the many professional activities in various regions, fitting actual AE fee histories of various project sizes and types to general curves of acceptable fee parameters, testify to the ingenuity that can be brought to bear on the empirical wedding of essentially time-based data (all fees really are such) to clients' ready understanding of (and some laws' insistence upon) a fee stated as a per cent of construction project cost. Here is no plea for that particular approach, but it does encourage the hope that, as fears subside and common sense prevails, the task of identifying and paying for professional services seems less than insurmountable.

Whether the percentage method or the more logical multiple of direct personnel expense method is used, the construction manager should make sure that his compensation will be adequate to enable him to perform all required services in a fully professional manner.

3 | ORGANIZATION FOR PROFESSIONAL CONSTRUCTION MANAGEMENT

There is wide acceptance of the belief that the organization and technical resources typical of general contractors provide a ready-made reservoir of firms capable of the management of large construction projects in the complete sense we now assign to the term *construction management*. It is only reasonable to agree that any large firm that has been in the business of assembling and scheduling the trade subcontractors and supervising their work and the sequence of their arrivals on the job must have a considerable capability in a substantial segment of the construction management operation. Further, the general contractor's familiarity with local conditions and subcontracting people, as well as his possible experience in special building types (say, mid-city high-rise) offer a ready leg-up to his qualifications for getting the job done.

But two facts must inject an element of caution into the assumption that even the best and biggest general contractor is ready for professional construction management.

First is the fact, already mentioned in Chapter 2, that the much advertised cost-expertise of general contractors actually resides in the subcontractors and is not an inherent attribute of the general contractor *unless he sets up the organization and personnel to make it so.* That means a considerable expenditure of time and effort in compiling records of costs and in setting up a method for accurate translation of those records into current project situations. Adjusting to current situations, of course, means predicting precisely the changes in cost of a given item, both with inflationary time since its last application and with location (since cost differences from one city to another are a well-known phenomenon). Also, there is a significant difference between "take-off" costing, to which contractors are accustomed, and conceptual costing of a project in very early phases. Both resources and parameters are different.

The second fact applicable to considerations of the contractor as construction manager is simply that the array of services implicit in construction management—and the professional orientation of those services in agency toward the client—are simply not part of the general contractor's inherent resources.

For example, the construction manager for a substantial project (say $15-million), for which construction consultation during design development as well as post-bid management services are to be provided, would need in-house capabilities in about 30 different skills. He (i.e., the firm) would need estimating and supervisory skills in all the trades, economists, scheduling engineers, architects and engineers for design comprehension and review of structural, mechanical, electrical and civil engineering input. Scheduling capability would require skills in CPM applications and computer programing. He would need skills in construction method and systems development for the professional application of what is now called value engineering or value analysis. And, of course, he would need the corresponding complement of accounting and data processing capabilities.

Any approach to organization for construction management must take into account three sets of conditions. One is the basic set of capabilities already existing in the firm, whether it be an architectural, engineering, consulting, or contracting organization. Second is the range of services considered to be adequate and essential to the construction management function. Third is the target size, building type, or complexity of project toward which the firm proposes to direct its practice.

We have already considered the practical ranges of such projects in Chapter 2, but the actual organization of legitimate construction management firms may differ in important ways depending both on their original practice and on whether they elect to practice at one end of the project size scale or the other. If an organization is already large in the practice of architecture and engineering, for example, it may already have in-house capabilities that make it more efficient to approach the larger works. It is not necessarily effective to consider starting at the small end of the project cost scale with the idea that progression to large projects is simply a matter of growth. It is, instead, just as essential to scale the management operation to the scope of work. Smaller jobs need more careful scaling of services lest they rapidly become unprofitable to the consultant.

In other words, the organization for management is itself a set of management decisions, and the ground rules for managing small projects are just as demanding in basic management skills as are those for larger projects. The numbers of people involved in the management operation will differ proportionately with the work load, of course, but also qualitatively in the array of skills and their internal relationships.

For example, even though a project may not be large enough to warrant a regular full-time field representative, that capability must still be reflected in the internal organization of the construction management firm. You simply do not hire a field representative on a part-time basis, and if you need one full-time on a given single project, you must have back-up field experience in the home office to maintain the proper management force.

The organization necessary for the proffering of construction management services is implicit in the statement of what those services really are. Following is a list of services gleaned from actual proposals and contracts current in the industry.

PRE-CONSTRUCTION MANAGEMENT SERVICES

As early as is practicable during design development, perhaps concurrently with the architect's commission, the construction manager should enter regular consultation with architects and engineers (AE) and with the project administrator or owner on all aspects of planning for the project. Pre-bid construction management services might include, but not necessarily encompass all of or be limited to, the following:

1. Advise AE and PA on practical consequences of their decisions and design options. Review drawings and specifications, architectural and engineering, for the purpose of advising on site conditions, appropriate materials alternates, construction feasibility of various systems and the possible design and cost implications of local availability of materials and labor.

2. Prepare periodic cost evaluations and estimates related to both the over-all budget and to the preliminary allocations of budget to the various systems. These cost estimates will be successively revised and refined as working drawings for each system are developed. The construction manager

will advise the architect-engineer and the project administrator whenever the refined estimate shows probability of exceeding the budget allocation, or whenever the construction time required for a given system is likely to prolong or delay completion schedules.

3. Recommend for early purchase (by the owner or administrator) of those specified items of equipment and materials that require a long lead time for procurement and delivery, and expedite purchases in general.

4. Advise on the pre-packaging of bidding documents for the awarding of separate construction contracts for the various systems and trades. This will include advising on the sequence of document preparation to facilitate phased construction work during completion of the design development.

5. Consider the type and scope of work represented by each bid package in relation to time required for performance, availability of labor and materials, community relations (an increasingly important function shared by the construction manager and project administrator) and participate in the schedule of both design and construction procedures.

6. As schedule criteria of design and construction emerge, the construction manager may, with the cooperation of the architect-engineer, work some of the design operations into an over-all CPM or other network scheduling operation.

7. Check bid packages, drawings and specifications to eliminate overlapping jurisdictions among the separate contractors.

8. Review all contract documents to be sure that someone is responsible for general requirements on the site and for temporary facilities to house the management and supervision operation. Sometimes the owner provides temporary facilities and certain furnishings for conduct of the job site management and commerce. The construction manager should ascertain that specifications for such headquarters and furnishings are adequate to the operation. Sometimes the general requirements are a separate contract under which temporary site buildings, general guardrails, some items of machinery, access and security measures are taken care of, either by a separate contractor or one of the primes doing other parts of the work. As early as possible, the construction manager should set up a checklist of such general requirements to be sure that someone is responsible for each.

9. Conduct pre-bid conferences among contractors, subcontractors and manufacturers of systems and subsystems to be sure that all bidders understand the components of the bidding documents and the management techniques that will be applied including any computerized intercommunication, network scheduling and cash flow controls.

10. Review stipulations of the project administrator with the bidders regarding the construction management personnel, services, control authori-

ORGANIZATION FOR PROFESSIONAL CONSTRUCTION MANAGEMENT

ties, insurance, bonding, liability and other aspects of the construction management commission.

CM SERVICES DURING CONSTRUCTION

The construction manager reviews all bids for compliance with stipulated conditions. He also makes recommendations for awards and may, with the concurrence of the architects, engineers and owner's project administrator, enter into the pre-qualifying and actual awarding process. On a phased construction project, he will coordinate the awards with the planning schedule and provide the following services:

1. Manage the general coordination and scheduling of the work.

2. Maintain his own supervisory and inspection staff at the job site as well as conducting factory inspections as required.

3. Observe work in progress to assure compliance with drawings and specifications.

4. Confer with architects and engineers when clarification or interpretation of the documents becomes necessary.

5. Obtain and transmit in writing to all concerned any contract interpretations where any possible dispute may arise.

6. Set up on-site lines of authority and communication to be sure progress of the work of all contractors is unimpeded and the intent of the architects and engineers is accurately fulfilled.

7. Set up assurances, perhaps in the form of organization charts, showing the project administrator exactly what on-site personnel and organization channels are provided and see that no changes are made without the written approval of the administrator.

8. Establish procedures for coordination among the administrator, architects, engineers, separate contractors and the construction management organization.

9. Conduct such conferences among successful bidders as may be necessary to maintain schedule and clarify any matters in dispute.

10. Revise and refine estimates as construction proceeds and as required to incorporate approved changes as they occur. Monitor estimates and changes to be sure that neither the schedule nor the budget is in danger of being exceeded.

11. Establish procedures for processing shop drawings, catalogs and samples, the scheduling of material requirements, and prompt cash flow as job phases are completed.

12. See that each contractor's labor and equipment are adequate for the work and the schedule.

13. Be aware of safety programs developed by each separate contractor

and especially those safety provisions for the over-all job as provided by the general requirements contractor. (The construction manager should be sure that his own commission language stipulates that this attention to safety provisions does not relieve the separate contractors of their responsibilities or liabilities for safety and/or property damage.)

14. Assist the administrator and the various contractors in the development and administration of an over-all labor relations and community relations program for the project.

15. Update and keep current the CPM or other computerized over-all control and be sure that all parties with the need to know are informed.

16. Maintain records at the job site and elsewhere including, but not limited to, records of all contracts, shop drawings, samples, purchases, subcontracts, materials, equipment, applicable codes and standards, etc. These records are to be available to the AE and project administrator and may become property of the PA at the time of final payment.

17. Maintain cost accounting records of all job components including separate accounting of the cost consequences of any change order and its effect on the schedule.

18. Keep accurate progress reports during all stages of construction.

19. Submit summaries as required, either by the project administrator or by the management process itself. Computerize records of time, cost and materials, so that print-out can be made rapidly on any classification basis required, including cash flow.

20. Review and process all applications for progress payments.

21. Review all requests for changes and submit recommendations to the architects, engineers, and the project administrator.

22. Implement any special client requirements regarding processing forms or job conditions.

23. Be prepared to supply any documentation required in the handling of claims or disputes (and be sure the cost of preparing any such submission is covered one way or another in the construction management agreement).

24. Advise owner to obtain from qualified surveyors such certified records of site conditions, elevations, floor levels, etc., as may be required.

25. Insure that contractors maintain a current set of record working drawings and specifications.

26. Set up a joint inspection of the whole project at some specified interval prior to completion, the inspection to be made by the construction manager in company with the project administrator and/or owner, the architects and engineers and other interested parties. This inspection and the final inspection should be followed by decisions on the part of all concerned

ORGANIZATION FOR PROFESSIONAL CONSTRUCTION MANAGEMENT

as to the most economical and/or expeditious ways of handling a "punch list" of incomplete and/or faulty installations.

Note that the construction manager's agreement should stipulate that none of his inspection work will relieve any contractor of his responsibility to provide acceptable materials or to properly perform the work in accordance with the drawings and specifications. Until such time as the lines of liability are more clearly defined, no part of the construction manager's function should be construed as providing direct supervision or instruction of the work or methods of the contractor.

SERVICES OF AE AND PROJECT ADMINISTRATOR

It is apparent in the foregoing summary of construction management services that the architect-engineer and project administrator will both gain considerable backup in much of the "chore work" associated with normal owner-AE roles in lesser, conventionally scheduled works. The AE firm principal, for example, may elect not to assign a resident engineer or job representative for continuous on-site reviewing services—although nothing should be construed as relieving him of all on-site services necessary to see that the esthetic and technical intent of the contract documents is being carried out. He may also be required by code to furnish certain on-site inspections of structural, electrical and mechanical items.

The presence of the construction manager also puts into better professional perspective the following familiar phrases from AIA and other contract documents: The Architect shall not be responsible, however, for constructions means, methods, techniques, schedules, sequences, procedures, or for safety precautions and programs of the construction contractors in connection with the project. All of those should be the primary concern of the construction manager and/or construction contractors as provided by the various agreements.

The architect's own job-coordinator (manager, captain, body-in-charge, or what-you-will) remains in unchanged, traditional authority with respect to getting the project designed and built. He simply adjusts his communications network and his own responsiveness to accommodate to the owner-PA-CM situation *whatever it may be*.

The architect actually interprets drawings and specifications and approves all manufacturers, materials and samples. He reviews inspection reports and decides all questions of design and of substitution of materials.

He reviews change orders concerning matters of design and engineering, estimates their cost consequences, and returns them to the construction manager for cost confirmation so they can be negotiated with the owner and/or project administrator.

He reviews all written guarantees, instruction manuals and similar data assembled from contractors by the construction manager on behalf of the client and his project administrator.

Where the construction management services are performed by the AE firm itself, it may be expedient for one reason or another (fee calculations, proposal or agreement clarification, owner's regulations, internal management, etc.) to identify the services as in one category or another. If so, the theoretical logic and listings offered here may serve as guidelines, but, it is to be hoped, with an overriding logic both internal to the firm's own structure and external to the particulars of the project itself. Again, it's all just common sense and professional integrity.

The role of the project administrator is implicit in the outline of functions early in Chapter 2. Just as no two projects are exactly alike, owners also differ in attitudes, organization and capability. Therefore, so also do the precise identities, resources and powers of their project administrators. The implications for "organization for professional construction management" are manifestly endless combinations and shifts in emphasis among all the skills and services outlined so far—and others that will emerge as experience develops.

Nevertheless, those four identities (Owner, Architect-Engineer, Project Administrator and Construction Manager) remain as a molecular constellation of roles and agency relationships capable of virtually infinite isotopes but sustaining a basic and, if you will, classic identity.

The diagram, opposite, is such a constellation. The circles are of equal diameter and overlap—not to show any ideal area function or equality of powers or "importance" (although who can say that isn't so on occasion?) —but to permit optically clear (and neatly square) straight line representation of the lines of communication and/or agency.

At risk of reading too much into the diagram, consider the cusps based external to the square. The Owner-AE cusp might represent the AE as developer. The PA-CM cusp might represent a mix of capabilities a single professional firm could offer (as some do) on giant projects for clients of limited skill-resources. The AE-CM cusp might represent a situation wherein only the cost consultation or other segments of the CM firm's capabilities apply.

There is some temptation to extend the straight lines to a whole satellite galaxy of consulting services, but this figure is intended to represent only the nucleus of basic team unity.

In some situations, there may be only three circles in the construction team molecule. For example, the "construction prologue" of the New York State publication "Management of State University Construction Fund Projects" has the following paragraph:

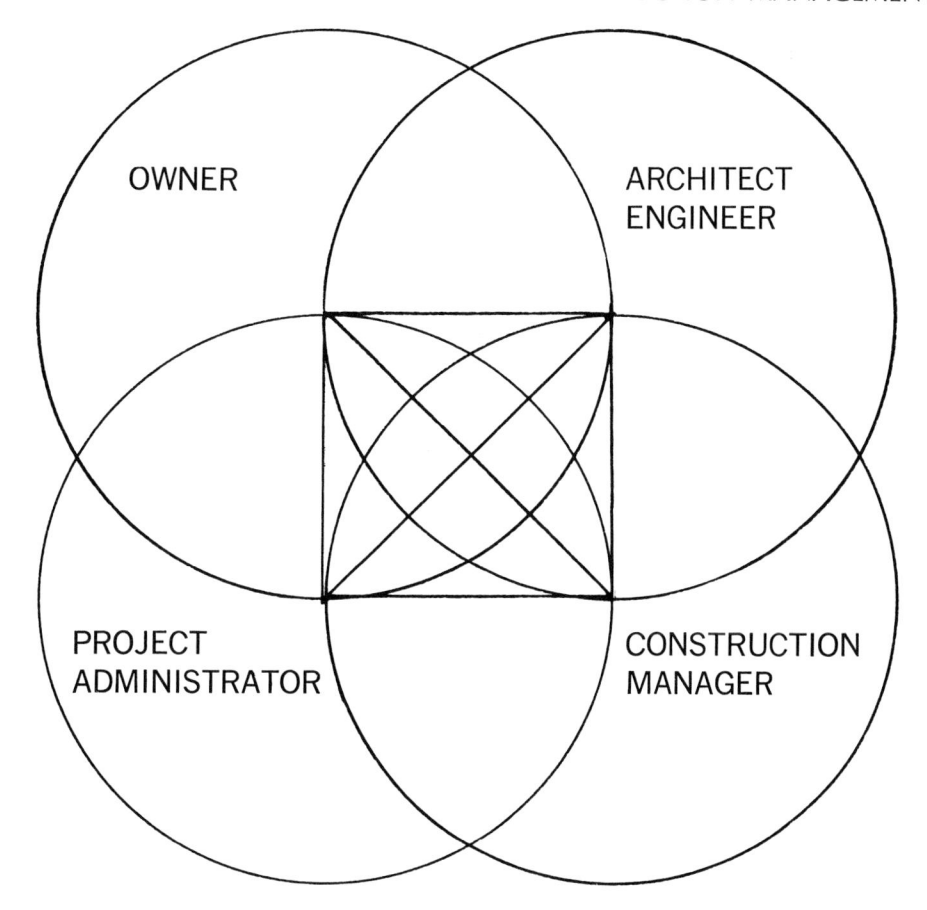

Four principal roles in the management nucleus interact and overlap. Two or more may, in fact, co-reside in a single firm, so the symmetry of the above diagram represents a balance of management function rather than the physical identity of individuals. Areas of overlap and central relationships are not fixed.

"In attempting to meet these objectives [quality architecture, on time, within budget] during design, the Fund has emphasized the architect's responsibility for project development and management. Therefore, it is imperative that the responsibility for the management of projects under construction also rests squarely with the architect."

So, the AE and CM circles might coincide in that case, with the owner circle marked SUNY and the PA circle marked SUCF. The AE-CM firm's organization will be more clearly implicit in discussion of project examples in later chapters. There is also, of course, the identity of PA and Owner which can sometimes coincide in a single circle.

ORGANIZATION CHARTS AND FORMS

There is no such thing as an ideal organization chart. Most such exhibits are either over-simplified to the point where important lines of communication are lost—or the chart becomes so complex as to be indecipherable. Nevertheless, it is possible to demonstrate some of the echelons of operation, and

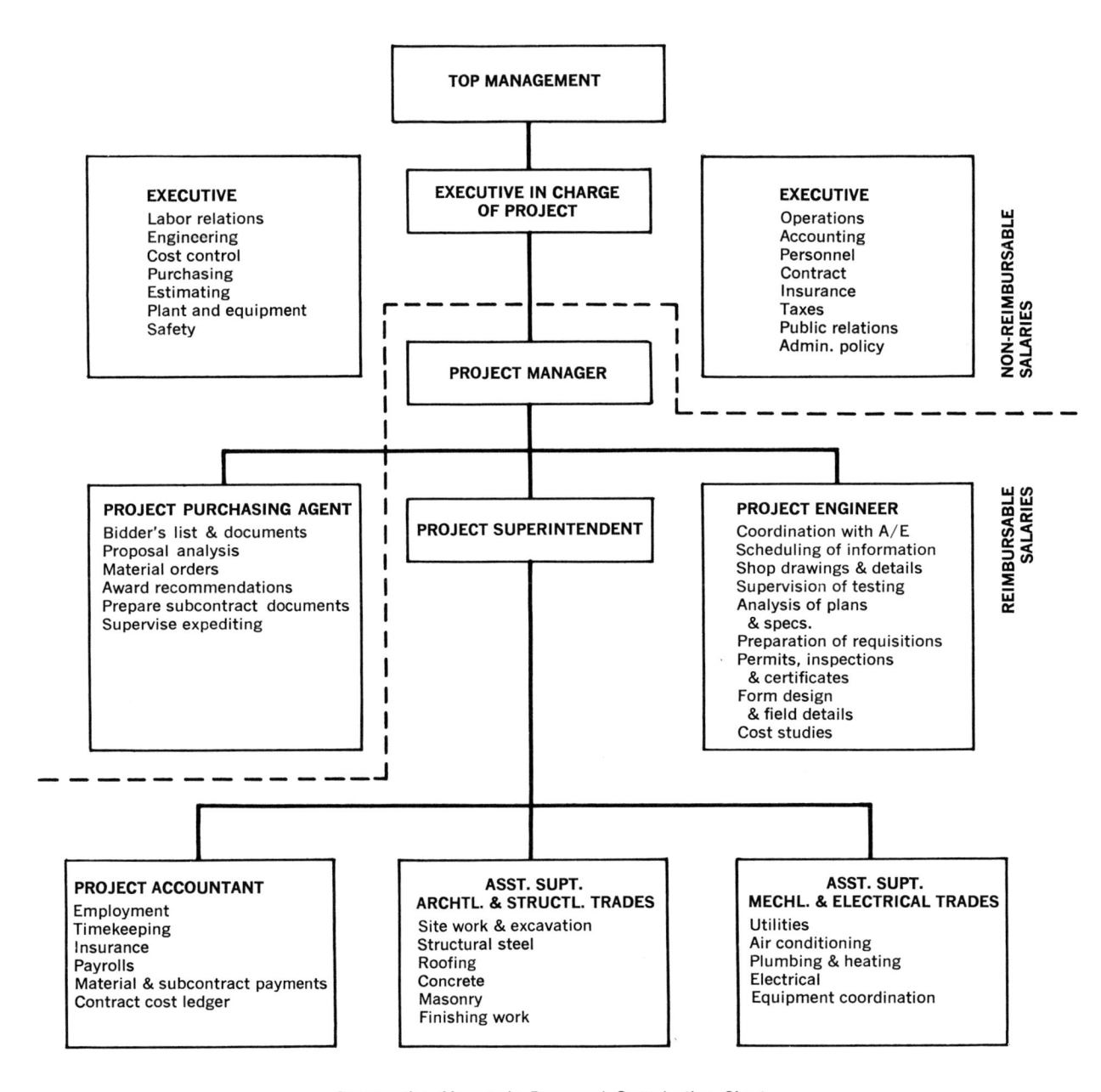

```
                          ┌──────────────────┐
                          │  TOP MANAGEMENT  │
                          └────────┬─────────┘
                                   │
  ┌──────────────────┐    ┌────────┴─────────┐    ┌──────────────────┐
  │    EXECUTIVE     │    │ EXECUTIVE IN     │    │    EXECUTIVE     │
  │  Labor relations │    │ CHARGE OF        │    │  Operations      │
  │  Engineering     │    │ PROJECT          │    │  Accounting      │
  │  Cost control    │    └────────┬─────────┘    │  Personnel       │
  │  Purchasing      │             │              │  Contract        │
  │  Estimating      │             │              │  Insurance       │
  │  Plant and       │             │              │  Taxes           │
  │   equipment      │             │              │  Public relations│
  │  Safety          │    ┌────────┴─────────┐    │  Admin. policy   │
  └──────────────────┘    │ PROJECT MANAGER  │    └──────────────────┘
                          └────────┬─────────┘
```

NON-REIMBURSABLE SALARIES

REIMBURSABLE SALARIES

PROJECT PURCHASING AGENT	PROJECT SUPERINTENDENT	PROJECT ENGINEER

Bidder's list & documents
Proposal analysis
Material orders
Award recommendations
Prepare subcontract documents
Supervise expediting
		Coordination with A/E
		Scheduling of information
		Shop drawings & details
		Supervision of testing
		Analysis of plans
		  & specs.
		Preparation of requisitions
		Permits, inspections
		  & certificates
		Form design
		  & field details
		Cost studies

PROJECT ACCOUNTANT	ASST. SUPT. ARCHTL. & STRUCTL. TRADES	ASST. SUPT. MECHL. & ELECTRICAL TRADES
Employment Timekeeping Insurance Payrolls Material & subcontract payments Contract cost ledger	Site work & excavation Structural steel Roofing Concrete Masonry Finishing work	Utilities Air conditioning Plumbing & heating Electrical Equipment coordination

Construction Manager's Personnel Organization Chart

some of the services performed on a prototype project under a construction management contract stipulating normally reimbursable salaries. The chart shown here is adapted from an illustration attributed to Turner Construction Company which appears in a 1970 master's thesis submitted by James I. Lammers to the faculty at the School of Architecture at Columbia University.

The purpose is not to imply that every construction management firm should go forth and do likewise—nor to imply that this represents the full gamut of Turner's eminently qualified resources. It simply indicates the ideological line of difference between ordinarily reimbursable salaries and others. Not every management contract will retain the full roster of salaries shown, but the separation does indicate the kinds of personnel who may be stipulated by the client as reimbursable.

While there is a fairly clear-cut ethical and procedural approach to the offering of professional services in construction management, the organizational requirements and the details of realignment of professional habits of work call for honest, on-the-job research. This is not for the purpose of confirming the judgments already made as to the necessity for application of these procedures. It is, instead, the rational testing of details of method to increase the effectiveness of any firm developing professional capabilities in this field. It is to avoid the errors of using one-time success as the pattern of all future endeavor. The virtually infinite variety of client organization, program, and both architectural and physical options that apply in today's practice call for an open-minded search, rather than easy acceptance of success before methods can be certified as proper. In one of his talks on construction management, Philip J. Meathe, Jr., president of Smith, Hinchman and Grylls, said: "When a firm is entering a new arena, unless it is able to entertain new ideas, it is more than likely to founder on the shoals of past success." Portions of the next chapter on project anatomy are also indebted to Mr. Meathe's descriptions of the multiple bid process.

4 | ANATOMY OF A PROJECT

In any architectural project, there is an essential series of events. On a typical $8-to-$12-million job, for example, there might be the following familiar nine events: 1) The architect's commission, 2) program analysis, 3) schematic design, 4) the design manual or preliminaries, 5) working drawings and other contract documents, 6) advertising for bids, 7) the bid opening, 8) the construction award and 9) the construction of the project itself.

If all goes well, this sequence, performed conventionally end-to-end, represents about 42 months in time. As every architect knows, however, there are the normal interruptions for the client's review and approval in addition to the possibility that when the bids are opened the lowest bid may be substantially over the client's budget. At that point, a recycling must take place. At best there may be an adjustment in the construction documents. In some cases, however, the architect's contract may stipulate that he must substantially re-design the project, if necessary, to bring it within the budget. Such stipulations are typical in public work and are common in some private commercial projects.

In today's economy, there are a number of severe conditions. First, the escalation in cost by inflation alone can run 10 to 12 per cent per year. That escalation begins, of course, at the very inception of the project and continues through the last payment to the last subcontractor.

A second important factor is the productivity of available manpower. Sharp fluctuations in manpower caused by interruptions of the schedule through delays or improper phasing in the sequence logic can be extremely costly. Construction management plays an important role in this area.

A third problem area, closely related to inflation, has to do with manufacturing and subcontracting problems. The longer the construction project takes, the less certain it is that the early bids of subcontractors can be performed in the time framework originally planned for later phases of the work. Further, the ordering and delivery of materials from manufacturers are also subject to uncertainty, so the subcontractor has to add this factor of uncertainty to the normal profit margins of his bid. The less confidence he has in the management of the project, the larger that factor must be. And of course each added factor of every subcontractor shows up in the ultimate over-all bid. A similar uncertainty factor must be added by manufacturers who have to hedge against protracted delays in the delivery schedules of their products.

A fourth area of difficulty has to do with the bidding system itself. If a firm, either general contractor or subcontractor, has to commit its forces and its capital over long periods of three or four years, it has no recourse but a double gamble. First it must gamble that the forces of inflation, strikes, or unpredictable job conditions will not wipe it out midway. Second, it has to gamble on the skills of the management of the job itself in keeping the job on schedule over that same long period. The price of that gamble is reflected in every bid and becomes itself a component of inflation rather than a true reflection of the current market at the time of bidding. For example, if the contractor sees a lead time of, say, two years (out of a normal 42-month over-all project span) before a particular system on which he is bidding is likely to be scheduled for installation, he must guess blindly at such long-range costs and protect himself with a substantial mark-up. This may be as high as 100 per cent above the budgeted estimate.

At that point, the owner is forced to decide whether to initiate re-design, reduce his program or take other measures.

Further, the owner must take a new look at the over-all penalties of normal scheduling as affected by all the four conditions previously mentioned applied to all the processes and systems of the job. He may find that the "normal" 4-year design-bid-construct span is further extended another 2 or 3 years by end-to-end reviewing and approval processes in his own structure. Then the options for phased construction plus disciplined management of both the project and his own processes become virtually inevitable.

STEPS IN PROJECT ANALYSIS

A review of project anatomy and logic shows that at certain key points in the process there are accretions of knowledge that permit increasingly effective steps to be taken to shorten time and reduce cost.

When the schematic phase is reached, for example, there is knowledge of the program and what is required to implement the program. There is knowledge of the systems that will logically go into the project. Further, since both owner and AE will require cost estimates at this point, some of the options of size and systems development will have been worked out in some detail to be sure the budget remains a feasible one. There is knowledge, then, of how big the building is, the degree of finishes, the site conditions, the utilities, the heating and lighting standards, vertical transportation—a whole reservoir of information that relates to systems in the building.

This, then, becomes one of the essential points in the process of construction management. It is possible now to set up a list of all systems that will comprise the building. The estimate of building cost at this point is a summation of the costs of each of these systems. Further, these systems have a logic of construction sequence as well as a price. If the logic can be managed properly, there is a possibility for the compressing of time required for assembling the systems. Two procedures now become possible. First the systems can be arranged in the pattern of their logic and assigned a high and low estimate of their ultimate cost so that any budget overrun at this point can be reexamined in detail. Second, the logic of the construction pattern can be applied with management techniques to reduce the over-all time of completing the professional design services.

Once the systems are arranged in logical sequence, it is possible to set up an "earliest and latest date" for construction to start on each. This generates a secondary logic of design sequence. While this design logic obviously cannot be paced exactly with the sequence of systems construction (because of the interdependency of systems criteria) it is, nevertheless, possible to establish orders of priority and a framework of lead time related to both construction sequence and design staff loading. Many firms have been able to apply computerized variations of CPM to these relationships.

Fabrication time is another element in these calculations, since obviously a system cannot be put in place until its components have been delivered to the job. It is simple addition of these time elements for each system in the building that tells the manager what actions he must take and in what

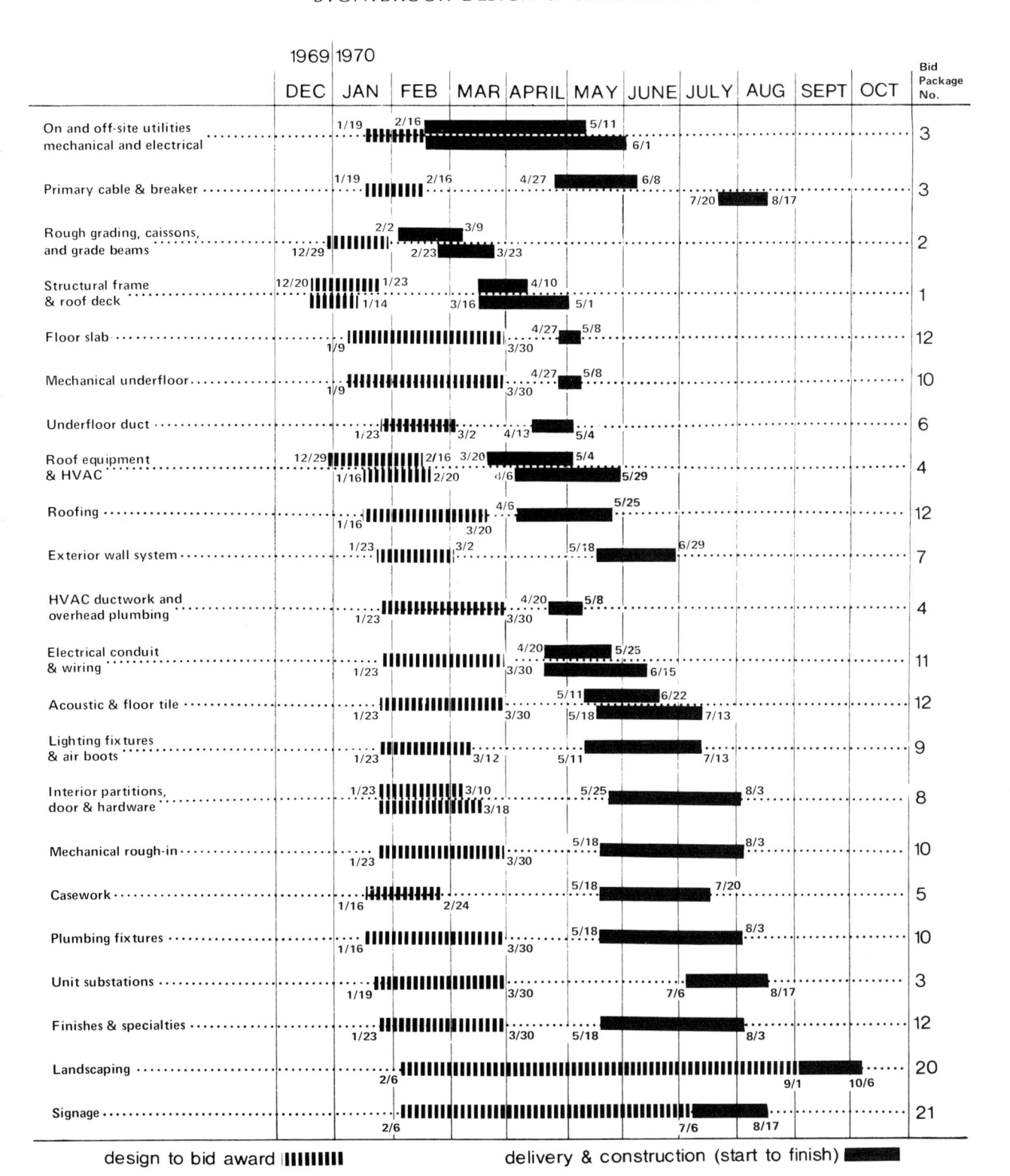

STONYBROOK DESIGN & CONSTRUCTION SCHEDULE

Task	Dates	Bid Package No.
On and off-site utilities mechanical and electrical	design to bid award 1/19–2/16; delivery & construction 2/16–5/11 / 6/1	3
Primary cable & breaker	1/19–2/16; 4/27–6/8; 7/20–8/17	3
Rough grading, caissons, and grade beams	12/29–2/2; 2/2–3/9 / 2/23–3/23	2
Structural frame & roof deck	12/20–1/23 / 1/14; 3/16–4/10 / 5/1	1
Floor slab	1/9–3/30; 4/27–5/8	12
Mechanical underfloor	1/9–3/30; 4/27–5/8	10
Underfloor duct	1/23–3/2; 4/13–5/4	6
Roof equipment & HVAC	12/29–2/16 / 1/16–2/20; 3/20–5/4 / 4/6–5/29	4
Roofing	1/16–3/20; 4/6–5/25	12
Exterior wall system	1/23–3/2; 5/18–6/29	7
HVAC ductwork and overhead plumbing	1/23–3/30; 4/20–5/8	4
Electrical conduit & wiring	1/23–3/30; 4/20–5/25 / 6/15	11
Acoustic & floor tile	1/23–3/30; 5/11–6/22 / 5/18–7/13	12
Lighting fixtures & air boots	1/23–3/12; 5/11–7/13	9
Interior partitions, door & hardware	1/23–3/10 / 3/18; 5/25–8/3	8
Mechanical rough-in	1/23–3/30; 5/18–8/3	10
Casework	1/16–2/24; 5/18–7/20	5
Plumbing fixtures	1/16–3/30; 5/18–8/3	10
Unit substations	1/19–3/30; 7/6–8/17	3
Finishes & specialties	1/23–3/30; 5/18–8/3	12
Landscaping	2/6–9/1; 9/1–10/6	20
Signage	2/6–7/6; 7/6–8/17	21

design to bid award |||||||| delivery & construction (start to finish) ▬

ANATOMY OF A PROJECT

order from the first day forward. The addition, of course, proceeds in reverse order from the end date of delivery back through required time intervals for construction, manufacture and design to a "latest start" date. With this array of schedule data, practical means of reducing over-all project time become apparent. The accompanying chart shows how individual systems schedules can be visualized. It is a condensation of a chart developed by Smith, Hinchman and Grylls for a $12.5 million, 190,000-square-foot science building complex at the Stonybrook Campus of the State University of New York (see *Architectural Record,* October 1970, and *AIA Journal,* May 1971).

BUDGET CONTROL OF THE PHASED PROJECT

The ability to save time by phased design and construction commits the client to early purchase and construction starts of certain systems well before the bids are in on later systems. If he is committed to a fixed maximum budget—as he usually is—he may well ask what recourse or assurances he has if at, say, the half-way point in construction he finds the bids are coming in substantially over estimates, and he cannot fund the overrun. At least under conventional methods he can abandon the project—or re-design it—before construction starts, and he knows what his completed costs are going to be. That is, he has bid prices.

The answer resides in two important qualities of the construction management of phased construction. First is the early and continuously refined accuracy of what we have called the "conceptual" estimating process (as opposed to "take-off" estimating—see Chapter 3). The client's, architect's, engineer's and construction manager's own cost data, contractors' and manufacturers' price information and other resources of the industry make it possible to set reasonable "high-and-low" limits on probable systems costs at the end of the schematic design phase. Second, the isolation of those costs system by system makes it possible to spread design flexibility throughout components of the entire project rather than forcing a massive paring job on quality after all bidding documents are completed and bids have come in over the budget.

So, the control point for the client's "go" or "no go" decision on the project shifts from the over-all post-bid point to the end of the schematic phase. It is based on a summation of "high" estimates for some 30 or 40 itemized systems and sub-systems. It further makes the assumption that subsequent cost developments, including the individually bid prices on systems, will average out well within the over-all "high" limit plus a conventional contingency reserve.

If bids on any one system come in substantially higher than the "high" limit on that system—and thereby threaten the average—the owner, project

administrator, architect, engineer and construction manager agree on one of three options (or a combination of all three):
   a) re-design the system,
   b) spread the overrun among probable margins left within other systems so far uncommitted,
   c) dip into contingency reserves to make up the difference.

At that point, assuming previously bid systems have averaged well within their individual high-low ranges, there is also a cushion of reserve represented by summation of the differences or gaps between accepted bids and estimated "highs" on those systems. That gap is not listed among the three options above, because it exists mainly as an indicator of safety or freedom from re-design; and at any given point in the multiple bidding procedure, the gap may be either positive or negative within some acceptable margin dictated by judgment, experience and job conditions.

An example of how the method works is tabulated below in simplified terms of five systems. Note that, since the method depends on management control of averages, the system estimates are in turn averaged as costs per square foot of the entire project.

System	Estimate Low	Estimate High	Lowest Bid	Gap	Cumulative Gap	Cumulative per cent of Job
A	1.00	1.25	1.05	− .20		5
B	1.50	1.75	1.50	− .25	−.45	12
C	2.00	2.50	2.60	+ .10	−.35	20
D	3.25	4.00	3.80	− .20	−.55	38
E	2.25	2.75	4.00	+1.25	+.70	50
	10.00	12.25	12.95			

The plus or minus tabulation of the gap is, of course, a convention to express the cumulative gap as positive for overrun and negative for under-the-wire. The substantial difference between the ten-cent overrun in system C and the $1.25 overrun in system E calls for the application of different options and criteria in each case. The overrun of system E is big enough to "threaten the average" and calls for serious evaluation and direct action as described for alternatives a, b and c above.

There are three important points involved here: 1) If the construction manager, acting as professional agent, has induced the client to make a financial commitment on the basis of estimates at the schematic phase, then he must do better than "explain" aberrations. He is now equipped with knowledge that enables him to make responsible correction of the overrun. 2) His own contract should spell out the limits of his liability in this area. 3) When the cumulative gap is still under the wire, he must do better than congratulate himself. He must advise the owner (or project administrator) of the implications of that under-run in terms of project finance. A few cents per square foot on a million square feet can mean a substantial sum in today's money market, and the owner is entitled to take advantage of the earliest possible knowledge of any reduction.

One of the important adjuncts to these considerations is the inevitably increasing role of the owner (project administrator) in the whole building process. He becomes more intimately involved, not only in matters of budget and finance, but also in the design as it unfolds, system by system. He is enabled to see the design consequences of his decisions in time for those decisions to have a balanced over-all effect on the quality of his project. In fact, this method will not work well at all unless the owner does maintain continuous participation in what has been called a "united team action program," UTAP.

The arithmetic of all this may seem to indicate complexity, but the opposite is true. The true implication is that management of the design and delivery of a building is nothing more than a resultant of three shaping conditions: 1) the isolation of systems that are needed; 2) the ordering of those systems for logical assembly; 3) the relation of assemblies to a time schedule for design and delivery.

Now, there are other and more important considerations in context with the anatomy of projects. If the method is nothing more than a means of delivering a quota of square feet to a given site at a minimum price, something is missing from the process. That missing ingredient is the professional guardianship of quality. There is nothing inherent in the processes so far described that should compromise the ultimate design in any way.

Two simplistic questions may arise: 1) What do the new methods do to client-architect relationships? 2) How does the modest-sized architectural firm fit into the new pattern? The answers are, again: 1) There are no "new" client-architect relationships—unless more intimate involvement of the client in his own building can be called such. 2) There are no criteria of firm size involved. There are only the criteria of awareness of the problem and professional respect for the complexity of consultation services. They may be enlisted (but not entirely performed) by one man—theoretically. But in a real world, one can set criteria for at least three men involved in evaluation of any management services commissioned in this field. They are: 1) a designer, 2) a field expert, and 3) a manager. Without at least acknowledgment of the need for the expertise of those roles, the small office is not equipped to enter into this arena.

PURSUIT OF THE GUARANTEED MAX

A variation of the system-by-system, design-and-bid approach previously outlined is described by Harry Golemon, senior partner of Golemon and Rolfe Architects, Houston, as serving both to condense the over-all project time and to permit a firmly bid cost commitment for the whole project prior to the beginning of construction. The method again involves overlapping, but with the difference that AE processes and construction processes are inter-phased on both sides of a single bidding interval that is moved up much earlier into the design development phase. It still takes advantage of the logic of systems sequence. The procedure is to prepare sets of a modified kind of bidding document comprising complete specifications system by system but only partially detailed drawings equivalent to preliminary drawings plus certain key details. These so-called "drawn bid documents" contain only sufficient detail to begin the bidding process. Hence, the method calls for a schedule of pre-bid conferences among designers and interested contractors so that the points that are important for the contractors to consider can be carried forward from the preliminaries into the "drawn bid document" phase.

All systems then are bid at one time, either by a single general contractor or any variation of the multiple contract process. The method permits the over-all design process to remain open so that any necessary adjustments of design to meet the budget can be applied freely to all systems in the project. The owner then has an assured (if not guaranteed) maximum cost bid by contractors before construction starts. (See chart next page.)

Many clients are eager for and sometimes insistent upon a guaranteed maximum cost quite early in the design development of their projects. This has worked fairly well in the past for office buildings and industrial structures where systems are relatively simple and cost histories are readily available. When the idea of the guaranteed maximum is carried into more complex buildings such as hospitals, laboratories and some educational buildings, the advantages of the guarantee as well as the certainty of the amount become illusory. As we have pointed out in Chapter 2, any guarantee of price calls for an added amount covering the margin of risk, and the amount grows larger as the risk increases.

There is a double-loading on the guarantee. First, the contingency element must be larger where the information available to the bidder is limited as it is in early design phases and may be in simplified versions of bid documents. Second, the price of the guarantee increases as competition shrinks. For these reasons, the "drawn bid documents" together with the pre-bid conferences must give participating contractors confidence in the conditions of the work, and the process must be held open to all available competition.

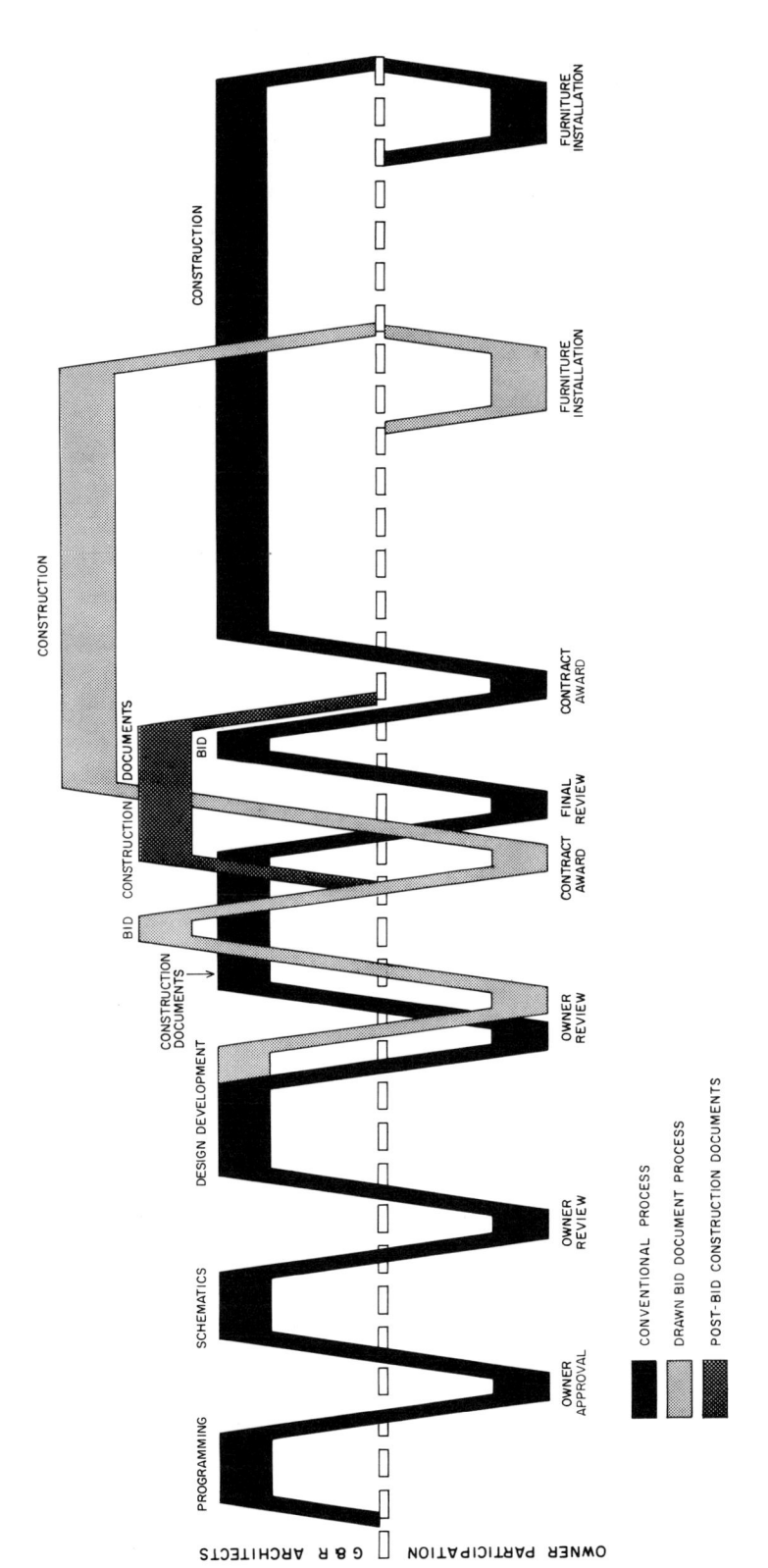

Use of "drawn bid documents" ahead of working drawings permits single bidding interval, early construction start, phased drawing completion, and shortened over-all project time compared to conventional sequence.

Drawn bid documents are not construction documents. The latter (i.e., conventional working drawings) are prepared after the bidding process by filling in the voids of detail not required for the bidding of the systems. The working drawings are prepared sequentially, so that, for example, the construction of foundations can proceed while working drawings for the later phases of the project are being completed.

To get maximum benefit from the method in terms of shortened project time span, it is important to develop the bidding documents on certain systems that are first in the construction sequence (foundation and structure, for example) to a more advanced degree, perhaps even to working drawings, so that the contractor can begin his work as soon as possible after acceptance of bids. It turns out that working drawings for those early systems tend to be the simpler ones of the sequence, so the pre-bid design time is not seriously extended by their detail.

There are two conditions of the design and construction industry that must prevail if this method is to operate well. First, contractors must be prepared with both the skills and the willingness to evaluate the condensed form of drawn bidding documents, and they must commit themselves firmly to the price of the bid at that point. At the same time, the architect-engineer must have access to a sophisticated cost control system that enters into the process at the very beginning of project definition, so that he can begin to zero in on final costs as soon as the scope of the project is defined and the general order of spaces and materials is established. If the early cost projections relate to the systems and to a convention of specification classification that is widely understood, this provides a format that translates readily into succeeding phases of the process. It is suggested that the 16 categories of the Construction Specifications Institute might be considered for this format.

By involving the contractor not only in the pre-bid conference but also in the actual preparation of working drawings after bids are in on the "drawn bid documents", many problems in field interpretation are avoided. Mr. Golemon points out further that the conventional working drawing that is prepared as a bidding document sometimes reflects the architect-engineer's notion of how construction is done rather than the contractor's more immediate familiarity with the construction process and his individual modes of operation. A judicious increase in participation by contractors during preparation of both the condensed bidding documents and post-bid working drawings helps to avoid recycling of shop drawings, according to Golemon. Another advantage of the method is the fact that it can be applied by an architectural office of any size to a broad range of project size and to either competitively bid or negotiated contracts.

THE MANAGEMENT MIX

In addition to the physical aspect of systems and logic of their management, there is another aspect of project anatomy that has to do with project history. That is, the generative background of each project is unique, not only in the idiosyncrasies of individuals concerned (clients, architects, engineers, contractors), but also in the complex of law and custom in which the project is required and takes place. All this affects the array and mix of management alignments and priorities as much as do the physical attributes of the project.

For example, any federal office building is intrinsically different in its construction management problems from any other office building—not only because of its scope, size, location and program, but also because of the special body of law, code and regulation that surrounds it as well as the peculiar gifts and limitations of individuals behind its genesis and execution. Consider also the diverse mixes of management implicit in these background circumstances for, say, the World Trade Center, or Toronto's Commerce Court for the Canadian Imperial Bank of Commerce, or a corporate headquarters, or a speculative development office building.

In spite of all these pressures for diversity, or perhaps because of them, the common threads of common sense become the warp and woof—the matrix, if you will—within which the patterns of management emerge. The logic of management structure remains consistent with identities discerned thus far. While the neat echelons of categorized services may be merged and overlapped by circumstances, the goals of project administration and construction management can be served so long as the principles of professionalism are sustained.

The following examples may help to clarify these points:

GSA STUDIES THE CONSTRUCTION INDUSTRY

Some of the effects of the physical and historical factors of project anatomy are underscored in various reports of method and project history. One of the outstanding reports is that of a study group commissioned by the General Services Administration's Public Buildings Service. This report, "Construction Contracting Methods," submitted to Administrator R. L. Kunzig in March, 1970, summarized the results of several months' investigation of current construction practices, public and private. The submission was signed by William J. Gregg, PBS Chairman of the group, Philip G. Read of the GSA Office of General Council, and Ralph C. Nash, Jr., associate dean of the National Law Center, George Washington University. Its purpose was to study "all reasonable means of construction contracting" to identify those which "would be most advantageous for the construction of public buildings." One result of the study was the commitment of PBS to the construction management method as will be described in the next chapter on clients. The following report on the World Trade Center is from the study and surveys the anatomy of that huge project from the management standpoint.

THE WORLD TRADE CENTER

The GSA study group collected a substantial amount of information on The Port of New York Authority's World Trade Center. This project is of considerable interest, since the World Trade Center was created by a quasi-public authority (operating with less freedom than that enjoyed by commercial developers but more freedom than had been available to GSA) and is the largest office building project ever constructed. This $550-million project consists of two 110-story office towers plus four smaller buildings on a 16-acre site in lower Manhattan. The whole project was carried out from inception to completion in early 1974 through the use of an extraordinary amount of budget surveillance and control by Port Authority staff and outside consultants. Elements of the procedure were as follows:

a. Selection of architects: The Port Authority teamed two well known architects in order to achieve the desired balance of capabilities: Minoru Yamasaki and Associates, who have a reputation for esthetic designs, and Emery Roth and Sons, a firm with a large amount of experience in designing utilitarian office buildings. In the opinion of Port Authority personnel, this team has produced good results.

b. Use of a construction manager: After the conceptual phase of the design effort had been completed, the Port Authority paid four general contractors $25,000 each to submit proposals to be construction manager for the project. After a significant amount of analysis and discussion with the contractors, the Tishman Company was awarded a contract to act as construction manager of the project. This reflected the fact that this company not only submitted the most attractive budget and CPM but was also an experienced operator of large building complexes. This work is being done on the basis of a fixed-fee of $3 million plus reimbursement of special costs and entails continual coordination with the architects, assistance during purchasing, supervision of construction, monitoring of the CPM, budget control, administration of changes, and some inspection.

c. Budget formulation: A major element of the construction manager proposals was a detailed project budget which contained analytical backup material in support of the various elements of cost. By this means the Port Authority obtained a substantial amount of budget information to supplement that provided by the architects and its own staff. In addition, budgets were requested from several producers of major subsystems of the building. The most important of these was the structural steel which comprises approximately 14 per cent of the total price of the project. All of this information was used to create a firm project budget which has been used from the inception of the project.

d. Phasing of the project: The project was broken into approximately 170 packages, which were put out for competitive proposals as soon as the design work was completed. The early packages, such as excavation and foundations, led to contract awards providing for commencement of work immediately after completion of the bidding process. In contrast, several of the later packages were put out to bid far in advance of the time when work would commence, with the result that the Port Authority gained a long period of time in which to evaluate bids and make changes in the products used or the contracting arrangement. In one case, in particular, this period of time enabled the Port Authority to handle the procurement on a multi-source rather than single source basis in order to effect a cost savings of over $30 million. The use of phased construction, of course, also allowed the Port Authority to commence work on the project much earlier than otherwise would have been possible.

e. Procurement technique: Although the construction manager prepared the bid packages and received and evaluated the bids, awards of the contract for each package were made directly by the Port Authority. In all cases, competitive proposals were solicited from qualified contractors and the award was made to the low offeror. However, the techniques used included several unusual features:

1. The qualifications of prospective bidders were carefully screened by the Port Authority prior to the solicitation of bids. Whenever a company was not considered qualified, the matter was thoroughly discussed with the company. Such companies apparently did not insist on being allowed to bid. As a result, bidders' lists were restricted to firms which the Port Authority considered to be qualified.

2. Bids were not publicly opened. Port Authority personnel have a strong view that contracts awarded on the basis of formal advertising and the public opening of bids do not produce the most favorable prices. As a result, although concerns were invited to submit competitive bids, no price information was disclosed until after award.

3. In cases where the low bid on a procurement package exceeded the project budget for that package, the Port Authority conducted extensive negotiations with one or more bidders in an effort to bring the price within the budget. These negotiations consisted of a detailed analysis of each element of work to determine whether bidders had based their estimates on mistaken assumptions. After such negotiations, each bidder was asked to submit his final price, and award was made to the low bidder. Port Authority

personnel were convinced that they would not have met the project budget had this technique not been employed.

4. The Port Authority also encouraged bidders to submit bids for alternate methods of accomplishing the work which would result in price reductions. These alternate bids were treated confidentially. In a number of cases, they led to awards to contractors proposing the alternate methods without competitive negotiation.

f. Controlling the schedule: The Port Authority used the CPM technique in a broader manner than is customary. CPM was extended to cover design, procurement and construction, and was applied to the efforts of all participants in the project, including the Port Authority.

g. Inspection: The major work of inspection for compliance with plans and specifications was performed by Port Authority personnel. This reflects the existence of a significant in-house capability.

h. Performance bonds: Almost all of the contracts on this job were awarded without performance bonds, in order to save the bond premium. Only in the case of the steel erection contractor was the decision made that his financial ability required the use of a performance bond.

CONSTRUCTION MANAGEMENT TORONTO STYLE

The following is based on a report by Robert E. Fischer in the October 1970 issue of *Architectural Record*.

When the Canadian Imperial Bank of Commerce had assembled all the parcels of land for a "super-block" development in downtown Toronto, management decided to call on prior "fast-track" experience and start construction far in advance of having a complete set of construction documents.

Consulting architect I. M. Pei and Toronto architects Page & Steele had worked out a large number of schemes that would have permitted developing the super-block in land-purchase stages; but it turned out that there were very few property hold-outs, and these sold their land in time for the project to be developed as a single complex. With zoning restrictions putting a ceiling on the maximum number of square feet of building, the final project—Commerce Court—evolved as a 56-story office building, two low-rise office buildings, and the bank's existing high-rise neo-classic office building.

Five years earlier the bank had finished a large development in Montreal, and still had retained a skeleton "construction management" staff. At first, they thought they would manage the Commerce Court project with their own staff, but very soon decided to have it done on the outside, because they would in any case need a general contractor to handle coordination of general construction and the usual specialty subcontractors. The bank, however, did maintain a very active supervisory role with its own staff of construction specialists. Thus there developed an over-all management role in project administration, provided by the client, and a construction management role filled by the contractors in concert with consultants.

The management mix for this project was unusual in that the client became convinced—at the urging of its mechanical and electrical consultants, G. Granek & Associates and Jack Chisvin & Associates—that it should divide the construction management into three parts: general construction (including structure), mechanical systems and electrical systems. Straight fees were negotiated with Mason-Kiewit, a joint venture, for general construction; with Sayers & Associates for mechanical systems, and with Standard Electric for electrical systems.

With the specialty contractors involved as management contractors, there was a much freer working relationship between them and the consulting engineers. This paid off in terms of improving the functional quality and performance of certain components. Example: a new type of trench duct for underfloor distribution was developed that has more rigidity and better access than conventional types.

The mechanical management contractor was to be responsible for expediting, coordination, project programming, checking, and also for such items as balancing, interference drawings and field engineering. The project was then split up into the following categories: 1) pre-ordered equipment; 2) pre-ordered materials, such as repetitive typical-floor ductwork and diffusers; 3) the sub-trades, such as insulation and thermostatic controls; 4) field contracting for piping and ductwork. The accompanying chart shows some of this organization.

The advantage of splitting the mechanical contract into many separate direct contracts was to gain lead time and to permit the owner, through the construction management consultants, to control costs. The total number of separate contracts in the mechanical area was in the fifties.

Bid openings were held weekly, with representatives of the owner, architect, consulting engineers, and management contractors all present. Thus all fifty-plus bids in the mechanical area were out in the open for all those involved to evaluate. Of course the engineers look at the bid-alternates from a technical point of view, the management contractors from an installation and delivery point of view. Much of the equipment could all be pre-ordered. Repetitive elements such as typical-floor ducting and piping could be fabricated off site.

To encourage the more accurate bidding of off-site fabricated items, the owner authorized the construction of mock-ups of various sorts, including an entire 50-ft bay of induction units.

The consulting engineers reported that they spent much more time on

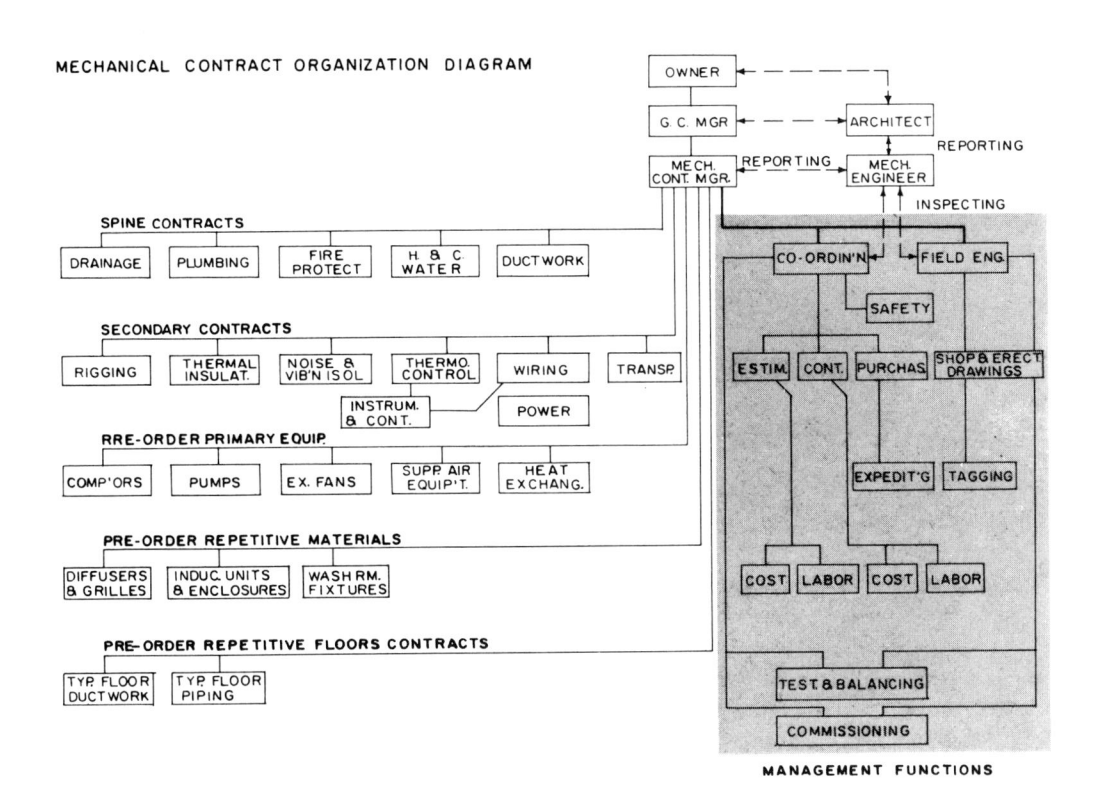

MECHANICAL CONTRACT ORGANIZATION DIAGRAM

```
                                    OWNER
                                      │
                                   G.C. MGR ─ ─ ─ ARCHITECT
                                      │              │
                                   MECH.    REPORTING  MECH.    REPORTING
                                   CONT. MGR.────── ENGINEER
                                                     │
                                                  INSPECTING
```

SPINE CONTRACTS
- DRAINAGE
- PLUMBING
- FIRE PROTECT
- H. & C. WATER
- DUCTWORK

SECONDARY CONTRACTS
- RIGGING
- THERMAL INSULAT.
- NOISE & VIB'N ISOL
- THERMO. CONTROL
- WIRING
- TRANSP.
- INSTRUM. & CONT.
- POWER

PRE-ORDER PRIMARY EQUIP.
- COMP'ORS
- PUMPS
- EX. FANS
- SUPP. AIR EQUIP'T.
- HEAT EXCHANG.

PRE-ORDER REPETITIVE MATERIALS
- DIFFUSERS & GRILLES
- INDUC. UNITS & ENCLOSURES
- WASH RM. FIXTURES

PRE-ORDER REPETITIVE FLOORS CONTRACTS
- TYP FLOOR DUCTWORK
- TYP FLOOR PIPING

MANAGEMENT FUNCTIONS
- CO-ORDIN'N
- FIELD ENG.
- SAFETY
- ESTIM.
- CONT.
- PURCHAS.
- SHOP & ERECT DRAWINGS
- EXPEDIT'G
- TAGGING
- COST / LABOR / COST / LABOR
- TEST & BALANCING
- COMMISSIONING

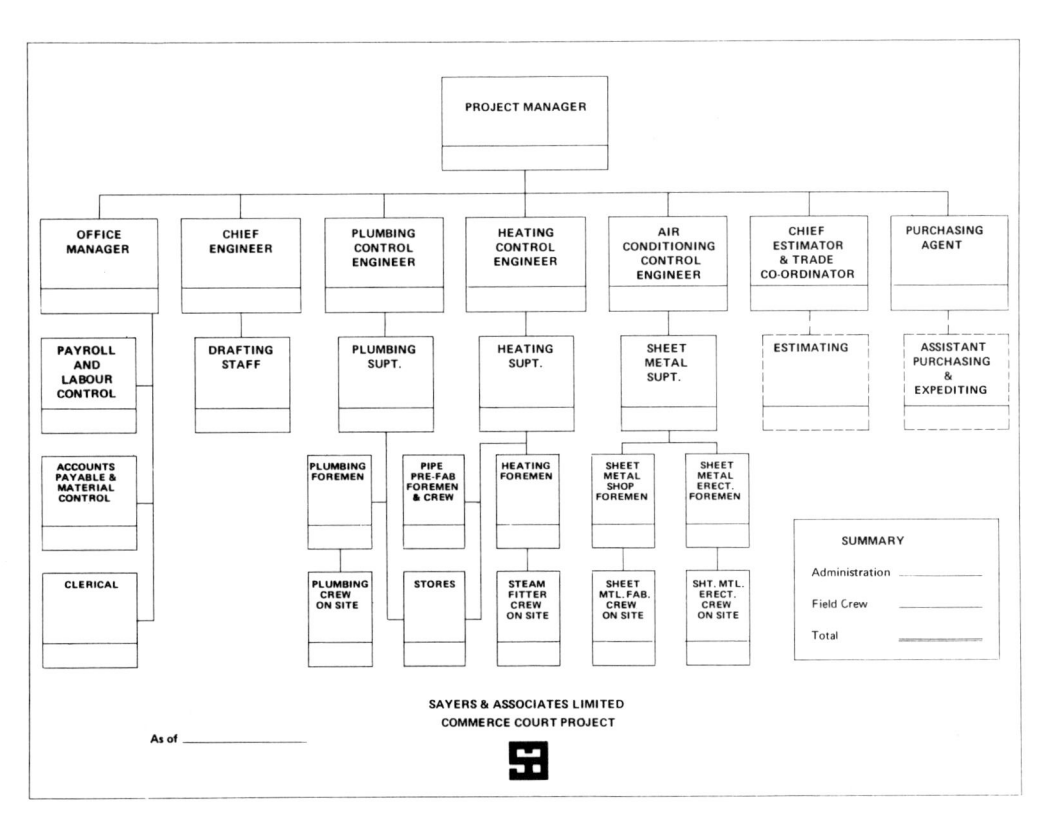

PROJECT MANAGER

OFFICE MANAGER	CHIEF ENGINEER	PLUMBING CONTROL ENGINEER	HEATING CONTROL ENGINEER	AIR CONDITIONING CONTROL ENGINEER	CHIEF ESTIMATOR & TRADE CO-ORDINATOR	PURCHASING AGENT
PAYROLL AND LABOUR CONTROL	DRAFTING STAFF	PLUMBING SUPT.	HEATING SUPT.	SHEET METAL SUPT.	ESTIMATING	ASSISTANT PURCHASING & EXPEDITING
ACCOUNTS PAYABLE & MATERIAL CONTROL		PLUMBING FOREMEN / PIPE PRE-FAB FOREMEN & CREW	HEATING FOREMEN	SHEET METAL SHOP FOREMEN / SHEET METAL ERECT. FOREMEN		
CLERICAL		PLUMBING CREW ON SITE / STORES	STEAM FITTER CREW ON SITE	SHEET MTL. FAB. CREW ON SITE / SHT. MTL. ERECT. CREW ON SITE		

SUMMARY
- Administration _____
- Field Crew _____
- Total _____

SAYERS & ASSOCIATES LIMITED
COMMERCE COURT PROJECT

As of _____

management than they had expected; reviewing multiple bids, revising drawings many times, etc. But, according to careful cost records, the client gained considerably in terms of costs related to the quality of the building. Moreover, the building delivery was two years ahead of normal schedule.

A BOSTON CAMPUS POSES EVERY MANAGEMENT PROBLEM
Development of a completely new campus for the University of Massachusetts on a 90-acre site in metropolitan Boston brought together an unusually large and complex mix of project management and administration problems. There were not only the physical problems of the site (a former city dump) and the social problems of its environs (adjacent to one of Boston's poorer housing developments), but the sheer size of the project itself (the largest ever undertaken in New England) stretched the capabilities of public agencies to the point where some access to resources of the private sector of construction management was necessary. First phase of the $355-million, 10-year project was to be a $150-million (later cut during the design phase to $130 million) six-building complex—each building by a different architect—a total of 1.3 million square feet, all to be designed and built in 33 months. The operating agency in this case was the University of Massachusetts, and the construction agency was the Bureau of Building Construction.

The master plan for the new campus was commissioned to Pietro Belluschi and Sasaki, Dawson, DeMay Associates, Inc. In addition to the six buildings, each with its own architect, sitework for the project was to be done by still another firm, Charles T. Main, Inc. The task of bringing together all seven parts of the first phase of the project and organizing the work of some twenty firms toward a completion schedule of less than three years called for a management presence beyond the scope of the BBC or of any single contractor. A commission for over-all management went to McKee-Berger-Mansueto, Inc. The project has required the professional input of a large roster of architectural and other consultants listed as follows: *Master plan team:* Pietro Belluschi and Sasaki, Dawson, DeMay Associates, Inc.; Bolt, Beranek and Newman, Inc.; Edwards and Kelcey; Greenleaf Engineers; Haley and Aldrich; Le Messurier Associates, Inc. *Project development team:* McKee-Berger-Mansueto, Inc. (project/construction managers); Chas. T. Main, Inc. (site development); and architects: Anderson, Beckwith and Haible (science building); Cambridge Seven Associates, Inc. (student college A); Geometrics, Inc. (service building); Marvin E. Goody and John M. Clancy & Associates, Inc. (administration building); Haldeman and Goransson Associates, Inc. (student college B); Harry Weese & Associates (library and plaza).

The management team made up of the BBC, the University and MBM decided that the only way to accomplish the objective within the time limit was to bring all the professional design firms together at a single location and to set up a structure of communication and control that unified the whole process. Communication dealt with the over-all vocabulary of the campus as a design presence as well as with the normal problems of schedule and cost control. The management solution was to set up a computerized communication system whereby all individuals within more than 40 participating firms (architects, engineers, consultants, suppliers and contractors) could be supplied with exactly the amount and sequence of information required for their own processes. In addition, the social and physical problems called for a well-organized plan for public and community relations.

The University planners (under Frank O'Brien, director of planning) had developed preliminary budgets and building programs before the construction manager was retained. The budgets were adequate, and although they were not luxurious, they were well planned and conveyed a clear understanding of goals and priorities. The function of the construction manager in this connection was to fine-tune the budget and relate it to a multiplicity of design options.

The project began with many problems of planning and design still unresolved; without a clearly defined role for the project management team; and with a site that had "underground fires, noxious gases, a thriving rat colony, large underground voids and distant bedrock," according to a report prepared by Bradford Perkins.

It was this combination of difficulties that created a kind of management triumvirate: the University, the Bureau of Building Construction, and the management firm. In this case, MBM acquired some of the roles of both project administrator and construction manager. That is, some of their decision and control duties were those which might normally be exercised by the client in more ordinary circumstances; while others were more clearly an input of cost and construction expertise as has been defined for the role of construction manager.

ORGANIZATION OF MANAGEMENT FOR U. MASS./BOSTON
Underlying the organization for administration and management of the U. Mass./Boston project was the idea that the design and construction processes should evolve and be recognized as a single effort. On this project, the management nucleus is set up with representation that unifies all three functions of ownership, design and construction. Thus, while the consultant manager relies on a large number of specialized support teams, there is a senior management staff which is concerned with all aspects of the project's development.

ANATOMY OF A PROJECT

The three key members of this senior staff are the BBC's project representative and the professional manager's principal-in-charge and executive manager in charge of the project. (Note that this executive is called "project manager" for and by MBM in the same sense as is familiar in an architectural firm's designation of "project manager." That is why the term "project administrator" has been used in this presentation to designate the "client management presence.") The BBC's project engineer, with immediate representation from the University, serves as the management link between the agency and the project, while the manager's principal-in-charge serves a similar function between the project and his firm's operating offices. MBM's project manager was assigned the day-to-day responsibility for the project management team. To somewhat labor our definition, it is this senior staff team that is our "project administrator." (See chart opposite.)

This team is located at a project office under one roof with teams from the seven design firms, their consultants, and the University of Massachusetts planning staff. This "one-roof" concept was developed as an answer to part of the communications and coordination problem inherent in having eight independent professional firms involved in a project.

Once the project office was established, the senior staff triad of university, construction bureau and consultant became the visible client presence as administrative agency. Management staff is organized into the following functional groups:

A. A design-management team under an assistant "project manager" for design. This team, made up of senior specialists for each of the major design disciplines required by the project, includes:
    a chief architect,
    a structural engineer,
    an electrical engineer,
    a mechanical engineer,
    a civil engineer,
    a specifications consultant.

These men serve as the technical consultants and design review board for the management team throughout the life of the project.

B. Seven additional specialists are phased in during the design period. Each is assigned one of the seven design contracts as his reponsibility. As individual building (or site work) project coordinator, each is expected to be the management team's representative and problem solver on his part of the project, as well as his project element's link between the design and construction phases. During design, the seven coordinators were responsible to an assistant over-all project manager for design, but

PROJECT MANAGEMENT ORGANIZATION CHART U/MASS-BOSTON

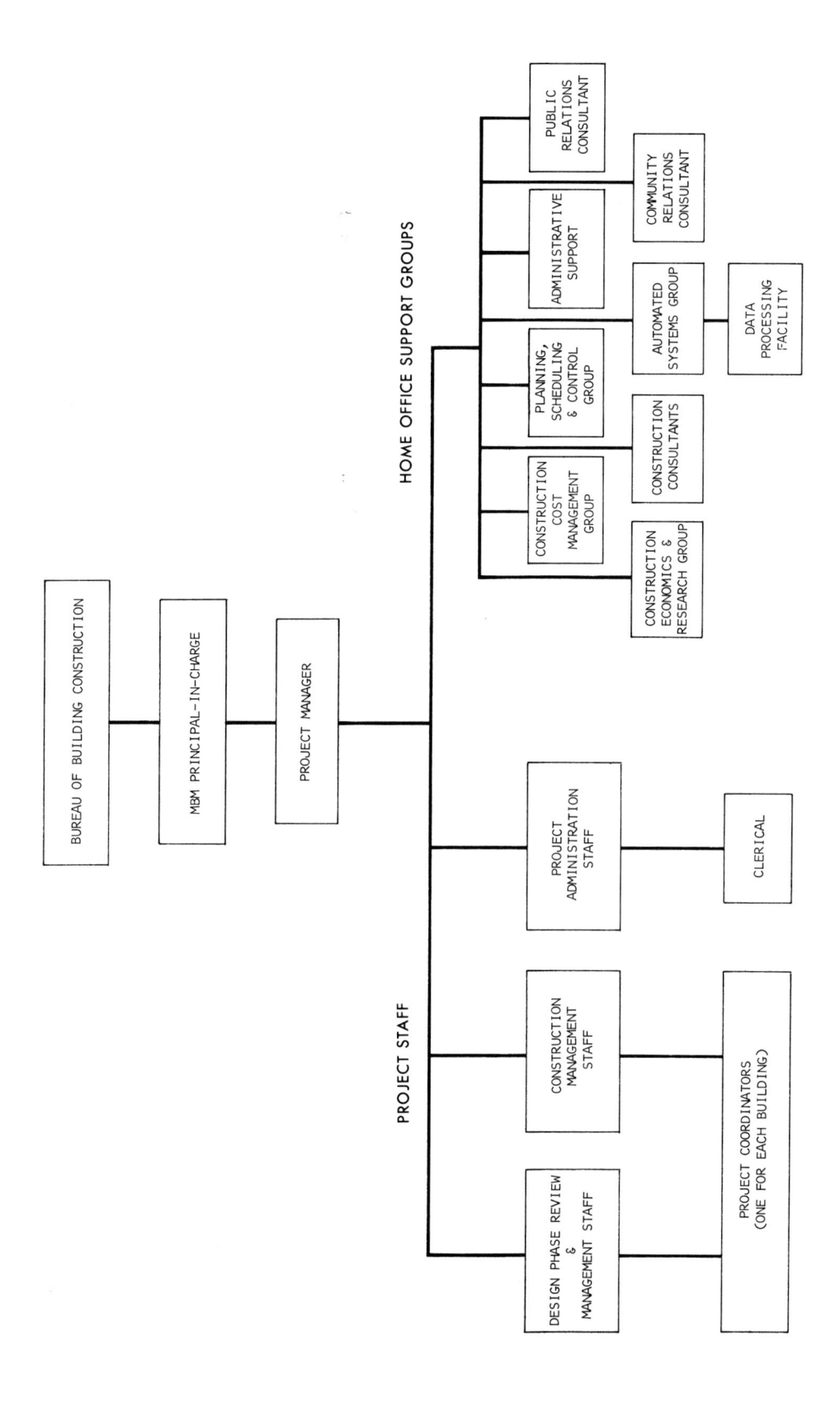

- BUREAU OF BUILDING CONSTRUCTION
- MBM PRINCIPAL-IN-CHARGE
- PROJECT MANAGER

HOME OFFICE SUPPORT GROUPS

- CONSTRUCTION ECONOMICS & RESEARCH GROUP
- CONSTRUCTION COST MANAGEMENT GROUP
  - CONSTRUCTION CONSULTANTS
- PLANNING, SCHEDULING & CONTROL GROUP
  - AUTOMATED SYSTEMS GROUP
    - DATA PROCESSING FACILITY
- ADMINISTRATIVE SUPPORT
  - COMMUNITY RELATIONS CONSULTANT
- PUBLIC RELATIONS CONSULTANT

PROJECT STAFF

- DESIGN PHASE REVIEW & MANAGEMENT STAFF
- CONSTRUCTION MANAGEMENT STAFF
  - PROJECT COORDINATORS (ONE FOR EACH BUILDING)
- PROJECT ADMINISTRATION STAFF
  - CLERICAL

once construction began they reported to the assistant project manager for construction. (See chart.)

C. A construction-management team under the assistant project manager for construction is made up of two groups. This team coordinates the many prime contractors and provides full time administration and quality control. The groups are:
1) The seven project coordinators described under (B) above, and one expediter who serves as an on-site trouble-shooter;
2) A group of six inspection specialists under a chief inspector.

D. A project-administrative staff under a project "job captain" is a support group of bookkeepers, secretaries, clerks, and a community liaison coordinator serving as the support and communications group for the entire project. This staff in turn needs the "home office support" of knowledge in:
construction cost management,
construction economics and research,
planning, scheduling and control,
management information system design,
general construction consulting (contractor claims, labor relations, minority training, purchasing, construction feasibility, and related areas),
computer programming and data processing,
community relations,
public relations,
administrative support (personnel administration, accounting, purchasing, and related services.

COST AND MANAGEMENT CONTROL AT U. MASS./BOSTON

Since the decisions that have the greatest impact on a project's ultimate cost are those made during the earliest stages of design, the project team very early initiated a comprehensive cost control program for use throughout the project. All members of the project team participate in this program. Part of it is implemented by the architect/engineers and their own cost consultants. The major cost control effort, however, is made by the architect/engineers and construction managers working together to achieve economical design and construction solutions. The most important elements are:
1) Analysis and adjustment of budgets for each of the project's major segments;
2) Market studies of the potential problems and opportunities of the local construction market;

ANATOMY OF A PROJECT

3) Development of a standard format for architect/engineer's estimates;
4) Detailed reviews of all estimates;
5) Value engineering of design alternatives to help architects or engineers in their cost-quality decisions;
6) Detailed evaluations of all bids and change orders;
7) Maintenance of a current working estimate that provides a monthly report on estimated contract completion cost vs. budgeted cost for each project element.

The consultant's actual role involved not only detailed cost analysis throughout the design phases of all six buildings, but also a deciding influence on the packaging of documents for more than a dozen prime contracts. This combination of cost control and bid packaging is also related to problems of a phased-construction schedule by which construction began within three months of the design team commission. The only way all these factors could be brought together was through a sophisticated system of combining the cost and construction progress control in a single computerized program supplemented by a programmed set of manually developed reports and communications based on the daily examination of data from the field.

The control system's output includes printouts of detailed project schedules in either CPM-network or bar-chart form. These printouts relate and update the project's cost; they fix important dates as a measure of progress; they print "hot lists" of critical activities.

One of the essential qualities of the computerized program is its ability to assemble the information it gathers into a suitable set of categories it serves. For example, the client may wish to have an over-all summary by cost vs. completion date, while the structural contractor may need to have a schedule of systems related to his own activity. The ability of a computerized reporting method to separate the categories of information into required juxtaposition is its major asset and, of course, is economical only on projects of extensive size.

FOUR CORE CONCEPTS OF CONSTRUCTION MANAGEMENT

In his reviews of the U. Mass./Boston project and others, Perkins reiterates four key requirements (he calls them "core concepts") for professional construction management that have emerged from the pioneering 3-D publications of Robert Hastings (Chapter 1) and throughout the applications and variations so far described. In itemized restatement, they are:

1. The owner must recognize that he is the key member of the project development team. Only he can select and organize the professional team, define his own needs, set his priorities and make final decisions. He cannot

delegate these roles, so he must have a sustained presence in project administration.

2. The project team must have all the capabilities required to deal with all the project problems.

3. All of these capabilities should be brought to bear at the earliest possible time.

4. The project should be regarded and managed as a single, integrated and continuous process from programming through design and delivery.

MANAGEMENT CONTRACTING AT THE UNIVERSITY OF CALIFORNIA

In a continuing search for more efficient and less costly methods for obtaining new buildings, the University of California began in 1968 to explore a concept called Management Contracting. The system has related to the ideas of value engineering, but is adapted to the particular circumstances of California law as it applies to public building.

The University's Management Contracting System seeks to enlist the expertise of contractors early in the design development without the sacrifice of the so-called safeguards of competitive bidding as required by California public agencies. The method is a rather involved procedure for pre-qualification of interested contractors, solicitation of competitive bids from those contractors, and utilization of the winning contractor's cost expertise in development of working drawings. The system permits a modified version of phased construction to take place.

The U. Cal. method differs from a traditional lump sum method in that the contractor is brought into the building project at the completion of preliminary plans. He then provides cost information from time to time during development of working drawings. The drawings are completed in a logical sequence so that construction can proceed prior to completion of all drawings for all systems. As the construction documents are completed for various phases of the work, the contractor obtains competitive subcontract bids for each trade. When the full set of construction documents nears completion, the general contractor converts his previous estimates into a Guaranteed Outside Price based on the subcontract bids. This price is subject to revision only by authorized change orders affecting the scope of the work. If the final construction cost, including fees, exceeds the Guaranteed Outside Price, the University pays only the amount of the guaranty. If the final cost is less than the guaranty price, the difference is shared by the University and the contractor in a specified proportion.

One of the legal difficulties in setting up the system was that pre-qualification of the general contractors had to be accomplished under publicly advertised competition. This was accomplished through a public advertisement called, "A Notice to Contractors," whereby all interested contractors were invited to submit financial and insurance information about their own firms. This information was then evaluated through a rather involved point system. Under this system contractors scoring over a certain minimum are thereby pre-qualified to receive bidding documents. The pre-qualification forms are seven pages of questions covering the size and current operating situation of the responding contractor.

The third document in the method is an Advertisement for Bids calling for proposals from pre-qualified contractors in terms of their expected percentage fees, sharing of savings and cost of pre-construction consultation. These bids include a base percentage fee covering work performed by the contractor's own forces and another fee covering work performed by subcontractors, the cost of the performance bond, workman's compensation, etc.

The contractors' bid proposals are then evaluated on a worksheet by which each contractor's bid percentages are converted to dollar values for the project in order to determine the low bidder. The contractor whose bid shows the lowest net cost to the University is considered the low bidder. A second post-bid evaluation can be applied to the low bidder if there is still some question as to his ability to perform. A footnote to a report by James F. Abbott describing this method states: "The contractor's post bid evaluation is more subjective than the prequalification procedure. Public agencies interested in using it may therefore wish to consult legal counsel prior to its use." The Management Contracting method was used for the Residence Hall for the John Muir College at the University of California, San Diego campus. This project also used another experimental approach called the University Residential Building System (URBS). During the developmental period of applying the Management Contract System to the Muir dormitories, the Abbott report states, "considerable concern was felt that the URBS experimental concept might increase the general contractor's fee on a subcontractor's work. This concern was dispelled when the G. L. Cory Company (the winning contractor) bid the same for both the URBS component contractors and the other subcontractors."

In submitting his report on this method to the University, James F. Abbott, at that time coordinator of construction and maintenance, acknowledges the contributions of the University staff, including R. Clayton Kantz, project director for building systems, and Hans G. R. Schickele, principal architect.

5 | CLIENTS: PUBLIC AND PRIVATE

Reference has been made to the multiple client, that is, the corporation, the school board, the hospital board, the public bureau, etc., and the problems of sustaining the one-to-one architect-client relationship. The following examples demonstrate some of the ways in which an approach is made to that relationship.

GENERAL SERVICES ADMINISTRATION: THE GIANT CLIENT
The Public Buildings Service of the General Services Administration conducted a three-year survey of construction methods (see Chapter 4, section on the World Trade Center). Based on their findings, GSA has decided to proceed with the use of construction managers in the planning, design and construction of new buildings over $5 million in cost. Procedures for the selection of construction managers and the awarding of professional management contracts by PBS have been carefully drafted, and a proposed format

for the contract sets forth the functions of the construction manager. Many of the numbered items in Chapter 3 were derived from that document.

The construction manager is defined by the GSA study as "a prime contractor for professional services, who will work with PBS and the architect to formulate the project budget, furnish the architect with information on construction technology and market conditions, to insure that building design stays within the budget, manage the procurement effort, supervise the construction of the building, and provide, if desired, a wide range of other services. In order to discharge these responsibilities, he will be required to have a strong in-house capability that includes engineering, budgeting, cost estimating, scheduling, purchasing, inspection, management and labor relations personnel. To be considered qualified as a construction manager, a concern must have a record of successful performance in both the management of construction and the furnishing of professional services during design."

The construction manager will operate as a member of a team with the PBS project manager and the architect. The terminology of the documents defining the scope of work of these team members will undoubtedly have a strong effect in generalizing the terms used in this field by other practitioners. The "project manager," in PBS terms, is the in-house client specialist who pilots the project through processes of the bureau and provides a one-voice communication between the client and construction project team. This is the individual we have called "project administrator" to avoid the use of the term "project manager" that is frequently applied to other individuals and functions in the design and construction process. Following is a summary of the GSA discussion of the management team and the PBS procedures.

The use of a construction manager, in combination with a phased, multi-contract system of construction, substantially alters the role of the general contractor. In some cases, the general contractor acts in a professional role as construction manager. In others, he will administer one or more "packages" of system subcontracts. In any case, says GSA, the legal requirements for competitive bidding are retained, since all major segments of the work will be procured on a competitively bid basis.

A close cooperative working relationship will exist between the architect and the construction manager. Differences of opinion will be resolved expeditiously by the PBS project manager having total responsibility for performance of the project. Management of construction, including adherence to project schedules, is a primary responsibility of the construction manager, subject to necessary decisions by the PBS project manager, on such matters as issuance of changes, settlement of large dollar changes as recommended by the construction manager, and interpretations of documents.

CLIENTS: PUBLIC AND PRIVATE

PBS PROCEDURES FOR SELECTION AND AGREEMENT

Since publication of the March 1970 study previously cited (page 46 e.s.), the General Services Administration's Public Buildings Service has conducted many seminars and much research in developing the ideas of construction management across a broad front of policy and technique. A summary of findings is set forth in a 60-page manual, *The GSA System for Construction Management* dated April 1975.

One change from prior attitudes seems to be an implicit shift from what some have alleged to be a commitment to former general contractors in the role of construction manager. A statement, under the subheading "Problem areas," says "interested A-E's should have a capability to direct, coordinate and expedite day to day field operations of many separate contractors if they seek GSA construction management contracts." Another warning in this same section is that "buying-in, at or below cost, by firms or joint ventures that want to get a foothold in the expanding field of construction management is detrimental to overall services." Another: "meaningful involvement of CM's in design development has been difficult to achieve. For many CM's this is a new responsibility for which they must develop the experience and expertise." And, again, germane to the design phase: "conceptual estimating where design approaches are comparatively explored and evaluated is an area in which CM's should develop more expertise."

The general introduction regards the working relationship among owner, architect-engineer, and contractor as a "new team approach" that now makes possible the early formulation of critical project decisions on a more coordinated and objective basis while drawing on the "uninhibited experience and knowledge of the architect-engineer and the construction manager, both of whom are pledged to the owner's best interests. The old antagonisms are laid to rest and a new cooperative spirit emerges."

Despite the implication that the CM contract may now be open to qualified A-E firms, there is no history nor statement of policy regarding the possibility of a single A-E firm, however qualified, to act as both A-E and CM on a single project. The book envisions "a triumvirate of owner, architect-engineer and construction manager as a team with no prime participant, only indispensable members working side by side." The architect-engineer is in his normal design role, but "with estimates and advices of the construction manager" is required by his contract to design so that the project bidding is within the established cost limitation. In addition, the A-E firm in this system "must package the output of working drawings and specifications to fit the most advantageous packaging and grouping of separate construction contracts selected, while working within a strict schedule discipline." The thrust of the GSA policy is to encourage, if not enforce, the multiple contract, phased construction approach to project delivery.

CLIENTS: PUBLIC AND PRIVATE

There have been some modifications in the GSA methods of qualifying and selecting construction managers. In general, the selection is based on a two-step process; first, an invitation to submit qualifications of the firm through response to a detailed questionnaire (seven pages in the April, 1975 GSA manual cited above) then a second invitation to submit a management plan with prices of services. These submissions are processed and reviewed by an in-house GSA *ad hoc* committee, and the relative weights of a candidate firm's CM organization, management plan and price are scored in a formal way so that the price itself is not necessarily the prevailing factor in awarding a commission. It turns out that the weight of the price constitutes about 30 per cent of the score in a given proposal.

Following is a detailed outline of the selection procedure as presented in the 1975 publication:

Project notice. When a project has been selected for construction management in conjunction with phased construction, generally those over $5 million in estimated construction cost, a CM project notice containing prequalification criteria is publicized nationwide through the *Commerce Business Daily*.

Request for qualifications submission. Under a two-step procurement procedure (1. qualifications, then 2. price with management plan) responding firms or joint ventures are furnished a Request for Qualifications Submission with the construction management contract and questionnaire.

Evaluation of qualifications. The qualifications submissions received are reviewed by an *ad hoc* CM Evaluation Committee of at least three professional employees of PBS, considering independent inquiries of references furnished and other sources. The committee then competitively evaluates and scores each submission.

Request for priced proposals. The offeror with the highest evaluated score for qualifications, together with all other offerors within a competitive range (normally no fewer than 5 of the top-rated firms) are invited to submit priced proposals, management plans, and resumes of key personnel.

The offerors are also given an opportunity to attend a PBS group orientation session on the contract requirements, prior to preparation of their priced proposals.

Discussions with offerors. Following the opening of proposals and review thereof by the CM Evaluation Committee, discussions will be held with each offeror concerning its management plan. Offerors will be given an opportunity to identify areas requiring clarification, explanation, elaboration or other modification of their respective proposals. Each offeror firm will be required to have its proposed construction executive, construction superintendent, and CMCS (construction management control system) supervisor in attendance and participating in the discussions.

CLIENTS: PUBLIC AND PRIVATE

Besides showing comprehensively how the offeror proposes to accomplish the project, the management plan contains a listing of "deliverables," 20 itemized management activities (review, reporting, buying, etc.) with price allocations for each of three phases of project development which make up the lump sum contract price. This listing relates to and apportions the deliverable dollar amounts at various points on an activity network diagram with both calendar and process milestones. The master schedule of the computerized control system will incorporate the deliverables and other pertinent activities of the management plan. A monthly invoice printout of the payment due the CM based on apportionment of the deliverables costs contained in the priced proposal will then be produced.

LUMP SUM CONTRACT PRICE BREAKDOWN

Deliverables	Design (D) Phase	D & C Overlap Phase	Construct (C) Phase	Total
1. General Management	$	$	$	$
2. CMCS Narrative Reports				
3. CMCS Schedule Control				
4. CMCS Cost Control				
5. CMCS Financial Control				
6. Design Development/Review				
7. Long Lead Procurement				
8. Separate Contracts Planning				
9. Interfacing				
10. Construction Development/Review				
11. Final Plans/Specifications Review				
12. Market Analysis/Stimulation				
13. Solicitation of Bids				
14. Managing/Inspecting Construction				
15. General Conditions Management				
16. Safety Program				
17. Labor Relations				
18. Construction Changes				
19. Construction Claims				
20. Value Management				
TOTALS	$	$	$	$

Note: The D & C Overlap phase starts with award of the first separate construction contract and ends with award of the last separate construction contract.

Modification of priced proposals. Offerors who elect to modify their proposals as a result of the discussions, can submit a written modification before a closing date established by the chairman of the CM Evaluation Committee.
Evaluation of management plans is then conducted by the CM Evaluation Committee and scores determined.
Evaluation of price. The lump sum contract amount scores are then mathematically derived for each offeror.
Evaluation factors. Each of the three factors (1. qualifications, 2. management plan, and 3. price) will have maximum scoring weight approximately the same with slightly greater emphasis on the management plan.
Recommendation. All pertinent data and the recommendation of the CM Evaluation Committee are transmitted to the GSA central office for final approval of the highest qualified construction management firm or joint venture.

Award. After review of the recommendation, the PBS Commissioner authorizes award of the CM contract to the offeror having the highest total evaluated score.

Type of firm. GSA prefers to deal with experienced firms or joint ventures currently engaged in the construction business, who are "abreast of the latest developments in this fast-moving field" and can furnish the broad array of quality services needed. Organization size is not a determinant; small, medium, or large firms being acceptable. In short—"it is not who will perform the work, but what quality services, personnel, and organization can be provided."

NEW YORK STATE: PROVING GROUND FOR PRINCIPLES

Procedures and policies of two New York agencies illustrate the divergent pathways by which the common goals of construction management can be approached. The State University Construction Fund insists that management resides with the architect, who is expected to call upon resources of the Fund and outside specialists for any help he needs. The Facilities Development Corporation stipulates that the construction manager for each project over $5 million shall be "a qualified general contractor."

It should be noted that the enabling patterns of procedure devised by public agencies, either national or local, have a common objective of overcoming constraints built in by laws passed when the construction process was more simple and more stable. For example, the requirement for completely open competitive bidding (which precludes any prequalification of eligible contractors) is ameliorated, if not set aside, by definition of the construction manager as a professional. Professional services can be commissioned by most public agencies without the requirement of competitive bidding. Further, for increasingly huge amounts of public work, the expertise of many large contractors remains unavailable because of their unwillingness to bid on public work. The device of calling on that expertise on a professional basis and for a professional fee has opened up that reservoir of knowledge. An earlier attempt to free the construction process from some of the limitations imposed by a combination of the single contract and its exorbitant bonding requirements was the division of the construction contract into four or more prime contracts on a systems basis (structural, mechanical, electrical, plumbing, etc.). Management of projects was attempted by assigning an over-all management role to one of the four prime contractors. This was a cumbersome system to administer or to finance because of the reluctance of any one contractor to assume the responsibility at any price and also because of the undefined scope of the general requirements that exist in any project. These general requirements include the safety and security provisions on the site, the delivery and storage of materials, temporary toilets and heating, etc.

CLIENTS: PUBLIC AND PRIVATE

The University Construction Fund maintains a considerable staff of people experienced in the construction field. One function of that staff is to implement the management tasks of the architects. Cost and technical information exists in the Fund as a resource from which the architects can draw. Further, the resources of the Fund include not only a substantial back-up of computer capability, but also a series of publications having to do with the over-all process. One such publication, for example, is entitled "Management of State University Construction Fund Projects Following Completion of Design." This is a compilation of specific information about the format of construction contracts, correspondence, reports, payments, etc.

While the Fund organization supports and even performs many of the functions described as construction management, it never interferes with the basic responsibility of the architect to shepherd the project from design through construction. Its agreement with the architect conforms with AIA documents with the exception that it stipulates a level of full time field supervision (and calls it that) for which the architect is reimbursed.

There are three modes of alignments to accomplish the management function for University projects:

1. Where a campus project involves several architects and a complex construction program, a construction manager may be commissioned to assist with the over-all project. Each architect still has the responsibility for management of his own section of the project, but meshes his work with others and adjusts his bidding document packages accordingly. The CM is an advisor to the Fund.

2. A management contractor may be called in by the Fund itself as a consultant to advise on bid packaging for an individual project.

3. The architect may have his own in-house resources for delivering the University construction project as has been described in Chapter 4 for the Stonybrook science complex, but this mode has not been used since that project.

4. The architect may have his own in-house resources for delivering the University construction project as has been described in Chapter 4 for the Stony Brook science complex.

The basic posture of the Fund in setting up its own routines and resources is that the supervisory role of the architect is one that should be sustained without fear of repercussion and liability. The owner, according to a Fund spokesman, has an inherent right to commission an architect to do the whole job. The plight of architects anent court definitions of "supervision," says this spokesman, does not mean construction managers will emerge as a separate control, because in fact they are the enabling instruments of a continuing process, the responsibility for which can only reside with the architect.

CLIENTS: PUBLIC AND PRIVATE

The Construction Fund has a classification of its own personnel called "project coordinators." These are registered professionals familiar with the whole process of architecture, engineering, and construction, who respond to questions that arise during the execution of the project from beginning to end. Each project coordinator may have a responsibility for several projects at one time, so his familiarity with detail of any one project is limited. He fulfills the role of communication between client and project similar to that described for the project manager (or administrator) of PBS.

The evolution of process within the Fund organization has been directed by the need for a sensitivity to practical considerations of construction. As projects become larger, techniques more complex, and time a more urgent factor, the process must still rely on existing capabilities for its operation. The capabilities of an industry that has been successful in the past as a fragmented succession of individual decisions by independent authorities either professional or contractual, is the basis upon which every construction agency must build its systems for coping with today's aggravated conditions. The University Construction Fund seeks to adapt itself to both past and future by accommodating its own routines to the capabilities of those who will be called upon to accomplish its work. In other words, differences in procedure derive from differences in people who are responsible for doing the work. If the architect has a problem of finding personnel capable in specific areas of management, the Fund can then be ready to supplement or advise.

The procedures for design and review of State University projects occur in eight steps which are parallel to, but not always identical with, the conventional AE process. These steps are:

1. A contract conference is held involving the State University administration, the Fund and others to analyze the program, estimate the budget and decide whether the project will go forward.

2. An orientation meeting brings together the architect and his cost consultant (either in-house or outside professional), the Fund's project coordinator and the staff of the college to review the program.

3. The architect prepares the program report and suggests some approaches to the design.

4. The architectural concept is further developed to a phase comparable to the conventional schematic in a condensed form. This is related to the budget, as are all steps in the process, and any adjustments required are pointed out.

5. A schematic report develops the concept further to a phase comparable to the conventional schematic design phase.

6. When the schematic report is approved, it is further developed into a "design manual report" which is comparable to the conventional final

CLIENTS: PUBLIC AND PRIVATE

preliminaries. The design manual is sufficiently well-developed to make firm estimates, and few changes are anticipated from this phase on.

7. Working drawings and specifications are developed and assembled into packages of so-called pre-bid documents following a 60% completion submission and review.

8. The bidding and construction documents are separated from the pre-bid package and advertised for bids.

UPGRADING NEW YORK'S HEALTH FACILITIES
Another New York agency that has been a proving ground for methods of maintaining architectural quality while meeting unprecedented demand for new kinds of health facilities is the New York State Health Facilities Development Corporation.

The agency started out simply, in 1964, as the Mental Hygiene Facilities Improvement Fund. It was created by the New York Legislature, on behalf of the Department of Mental Hygiene, as a means of accelerating the flow of money and construction know-how into updating old and developing new kinds of mental health facilities. Success of the fund's operation led to new assignments, first for the Narcotic Addiction Control Commission and later for general health facilities.

The role of the corporation is not only to administer funding but also to award architectural commissions and to manage construction of facilities for client agencies (the Department of Mental Hygiene, the Narcotic Addiction Control Commission, and now various city and county departments). An example of work on the City's huge Lincoln Hospital begins on page 71.

The procedures for selection of architects are flexible. There is no "approved list," so the whole qualified membership of the architectural profession is available to the program, as described in the January 1970 issue of *Architectural Record*.

The corporation commissions an independent construction manager accepted by the architect to work on each project. The construction manager is usually a representative from one of the large contracting organizations which have elected to participate in management consultation rather than bid on any of the basic contracts involved in the job. By law, jobs are bid under at least four contracts: one each for general construction, HVAC, electrical equipment and plumbing.

The corporation sought for many years to assign coordination of the four contracts to the prime general construction contractor on each job. This did not work out for many reasons: compensation for handling both the coordination of contracts and the general conditions at the site was difficult to accommodate in bidding procedures; sometimes the general construction

CLIENTS: PUBLIC AND PRIVATE

contractor simply was not equal to the management task; the setup was obviously prone to conflicts of interest in disputes among the prime contractors. Furthermore, as Campbell Reed, director of the AGC Building Division, has pointed out (*Constructor,* March 1972), the New York State Courts had ruled it illegal to require one of the prime contractors to coordinate the project. The courts held that in such situations the owner was acting as the general contractor and was, therefore, the coordinator. This owner, says Reed, then sought to have coordination provided by the architect, who "refused" so the owner "filled the void" with a CM. The result, anyway, was a chance to further divide bidding among many trades.

The answer to this quandary was the establishment of the construction management program.

As projects increased in size and complexity, difficulties emerged in obtaining responsible bids even under the four-contract system. The Corporation decided to make greater use of its well-developed construction management potential and to further divide bidding into as many as 30 trades involved on a given project. The process has permitted tigher project control and has attracted quality subcontractors.

One of the encumbrances on earlier processes involving four prime contractors had to do with the flow of money. Now smaller contractors who may be of good quality but not substantially capitalized have an opportunity to participate as primes and can be directly and promptly reimbursed by the corporation rather than being subject to the delays of transfer between prime and sub-contractors. The rate of payment has been accelerated to three-week intervals so that the demands on smaller contractors are alleviated.

One of the major advantages of the construction management operation has been the ability of the Corporation to involve the construction managers in design development conferences among architects, Corporation personnel, the client agency and various consultants. The advantage to the architect is two-fold. First, he gains assurance that his own administrative time will not be dissipated in coordinating and scheduling problems. Second, he gains some feedback of the manager's familiarity with local conditions in the region where the building will be located. This pertains not only to the resources of local contractors but also to the capabilities of local trades in using optional materials that vary in availability and cost.

In design meetings which (for a major hospital, for example) are regularly held at the New York headquarters of the Corporation, there may be as many as a dozen agencies represented, including the client agencies, the Health and Hospital Planning Council and the State Department of Mental Hygiene. That Department may be brought in at both city and state levels, because most large general hospitals now are introducing substantial mental health facilities. The medical personnel of the hospital will also be represented either by the administrator or various department heads.

This technique of large preliminary meetings seems cumbersome until it is realized that one of the most inhibiting conditions that has slowed the process of development and construction has been the increasing multiplicity of agencies and bureaus with some stake in the outcome and some responsibility for review during the development process. This overview process has reached the point where it is quite normal for a ten-year lapse between the emerging need for a facility and its ultimate completion. Further, the facility design itself not only suffers compromise for the mere sake of expediency in getting it approved, but is likely to be obsolete, or at best inadequate in scope, by the time it reaches completion.

One of the side effects of this conference process has been an educational interchange among parties involved. A city official from, for example, the Bureau of the Budget may not only increase his own comprehension of a project but may also get quick answers, without political repercussions, to some of the technical or costing questions that might have encumbered his approaches to a purely documentary presentation of the project.

The Corporation views the construction manager as a firm that is capable of coordinating a job on the site. While the same firm may have performed a consultant role during design development, it must convert its presence into a more immediate and sustaining relationship to the project during construction. The coordinating role of the construction manager is essential where the project is let in multiple contracts, although the distinction between his coordination and the various contractors' own direction of the work should be carefully drawn. The construction manager should not enter into a role of overriding foremanship, since the liability for proper performance of the work still rests with the contractor.

The Corporation has found that the role of construction consultant during the design phase is a new role for many of the contractors who have been commissioned as professionals in the consultation and management function. The effect has been a certain amount of educational process among such contractors, many of whom have observed a very real shift in their responsibilities and attitudes of agency toward the owner. The construction manager is agent to the Corporation in matters of work in the field, while the architect remains the professional agent in matters of field observation for purposes of interpretation of the contract documents. The construction manager is the owner's continuous representative on the site with respect to the work, but the contractor still has primary responsibility for work quality and method.

One of the dangers recognized by the Corporation in recruiting active contractors for a construction management role was the possibility that their commitments to other work on their own account might possibly reduce the quality and number of personnel available to the management commission. The solution for the Corporation was to stipulate that certain full-time personnel be assigned by the contractor to the management function.

Prequalification of firms for the construction management role is accomplished by submission of an outline of capabilities and resumes of personnel to the Corporation's board of trustees. From these submissions lists of qualified contractors are drawn up. The architect may choose from among three or four of these available contractors the one with whom he would prefer to work.

GIANT HOSPITAL TESTS N.Y. SYSTEM

One of the larger examples of how the New York State Facilities Development Corporation works with architects, construction managers and N.Y. City bureaus is the $135 million Lincoln Hospital project for which the office of Max O. Urbahn and Associates is the architect and Turner Construction Company is construction manager.

The Lincoln Hospital project, known as the Lincoln Medical and Mental Health Center, in the South Bronx section of New York City, is one of the projects being developed jointly with the City under revised commitments of the Health Facilities Development Corporation. It is a 950-bed replacement for outmoded facilities and is designed to handle an anticipated 400,000 outpatient visits and 200,000 emergency patients per year. The hospital occupies a nine-acre site and will be operated by the New York City Health and Hospitals Corporation. The construction management firm was chosen in accordance with procedures outlined in the previous section. Contracts were let under a multi-trade building plan, rather than the four prime contracts that have been customary on other facilities under development by the Facilities Development Corporation.

Normal duration for the preparation of documents for a facility of this size would have been about two and a half years. Under the accelerated method, they were developed to the first bidding phase in less than six months.

The design architect, Richard Banks, and project expediter Fred Montoya point out that over-all savings in project time are not simply a matter of speeding up the sequence of events from foundation to structure. In order to achieve optimum acceleration with maximum quality, the design for mechanical systems must precede completion of architectural documents so that the complexities of mechanical systems can be developed in phase with other architectural and structural documents.

The method, therefore, calls for the freezing of parameters and certain basic planning components of the architectural design very early so that mechanical and electrical engineering work can proceed with some assurance that the documents and capacities of their systems will need a minimum of adjustment in a later phase of design development. The mechanical and electrical engineers also require advance documents from the site developers, landscape architects, food consultants, and other specialists and consultants involved in systems that affect the mechanical and electrical engineering design. Early "quantity-scope" specifications based on estimates by a quantity surveyor (Amis Construction and Consulting Services) facilitated pre-purchasing and provided engineering designers with an inventory of available, pre-budgeted resources. This procedure did undoubtedly speed the systems design work, but it also introduced many occasions for conferences.

Bid documents are packaged by trade for fast tracking, and to avoid a large number of miscellaneous contracts represents a logical assembly of related construction items rather than a strict interpretation of trade definitions. For example, the package of bid documents for the electrical trades may include provisions for the electron microscope (which is Group I hospital equipment), while the package for the carpentry and millwork may include record retrieval systems, audiometric booths, etc. While conventionally there would be a separate subcontract for various components of fenestration, at Lincoln the logic of combining the glazing contract with the caulking contract and the contract for installation of sub-frames prevailed.

It is this overlapped logic of related systems for bid packaging that contributes to acceleration of the Lincoln job as much as does the phasing logic of systems development and delivery. Contractors who are accustomed to handling simpler trade packages need and readily accept some coaching by the architect and construction manager in handling these add-on packages.

The principle of continuing compatibility of these packages is a predominant concern. If, however, a system under consideration does not fall logically (or compatibly) within a trade package concurrent with its emergence in the design process, it may be assigned as a change order to a previously let contract for work that is in fact compatible.

This method of logical assembly and packaging sets up a requirement for the control of change orders, since an adjustment of a single item can affect the schedules and shop drawings of several other trades. Further, if the architectural drawings change while the mechanical systems are being bid, there must be a method for registering not only what the changes are, but how they will affect the whole interlocking assembly of other systems. The Urbahn-Turner computerized system of intercommunication is such that it can log the effects of one change as input to the full array of other systems.

CLIENTS: PUBLIC AND PRIVATE

There is a penalty attached to this procedure in that dozens of change orders add considerably to the architects', engineers' and construction managers' burden of detail. Serious design adjustments must be made to solidify the make-do bridges of early-on, best-guess design that have carried the accelerated process forward at the insistence of the client. But there is no acknowledgment in the fee structure to accommodate this inherent, patch-work re-design burden on the design professionals. This is one of the major concerns of those who propose to deal logically and reasonably with fee structures in this area. While it is true that accelerated procedures save the client a considerable amount of money (calculated on the simple basis of one percent per month in escalation, this could amount to one or two million dollars a month in actual cost for a given project), the added work, however clerical it may be, is a real expense to the professionals involved. Fees should accommodate this burden.

One of the effective means of making these interlocking requirements for observation and control work well is an emphasis on field management. This is supported by augmented field staff that monitors both the progress and the implications of design and construction decisions.

A part of the responsibility of this field management staff is to relate professional decisions to matters of union jurisdiction, to maintain supplier contacts (such as visits to the brick factory to supervise quality and delivery of their products) and to contribute expertise to special requirements (such as a change in mortar mix needed for the proper assembly of the specially hard brick).

The method of development, system by system and trade by trade, had some effect on certain of the design options at Lincoln Hospital. For example, the ceiling height, which (given unlimited time) might have been precisely designed to, say, 13 feet, was established at 14 to 16 feet so that the design of mechanical and electrical systems could proceed without the time-consuming constraints of overly tight clearances. Here, again, the price of speed is a value judgment the architect-manager team must make.

Another example of how the commitment to accelerated construction might affect design options is apparent in the design of the basement floor. There is a water problem in the site at the level of the basement floor. The solution that permitted both design and emplacement to go forward was to build-in the waterproof membrane underneath a flexible design condition in the slab. Two trenches traverse the 4-block-square slab at reasonable intervals and depths, encompassed by the membrane so that plumbing systems could be accommodated by drainage and supply systems without being locked into a completed design for the whole building. That is, the trench system, filled in by a layer of sand to hold strongly against distortions of the membrane, and topped off with a working slab at the final floor level of the basement, permitted the building construction to go forward while system design was also proceeding with foreknowledge of the underlying drainage capability. This was another value-engineering investment in design for the purpose of getting the job done.

Early "quantity-scope" specifications based on estimates by a quantity surveyor (Amis Construction and Consulting Services) also facilitated pre-purchasing and provided engineering designers with an inventory of available, pre-budgeted resources. This procedure did undoubtedly speed the systems design work, but it also introduced many occasions for conferences.

Design of the Lincoln complex began with the nursing tower because that space has repetitive elements and can be frozen early. Once the option for a 40-bed nursing unit is established, related nursing spaces fall into place in rather conventional ratios. This permits the packaging and pre-ordering procedures to start. The podium, on the other hand, changes both internally and externally, with events and changes in patient case-loading and methods of therapy that inevitably occur during the design process. An allocation of spaces to accommodate changes in the law relative to Medicare or to abortions, for example, could have a considerable effect on the ratios of spaces in the podium. This is the logic of last-minute freezing of the podium perimeter, although that has priority as a key point in the contractual process (i.e., as preamble to the foundations contract).

Max Urbahn himself has said of the pursuit of mere skills and speed for these assemblies: "Simple success in an enclosure is not enough for professional architects to contemplate, however complex may be the techniques enclosed. Mere acceleration of delivery, whatever the dollar savings, is secondary to a commitment to quality that only architects can sustain. There is a premium to be gained by acceleration that professional management alone can realize. But there is a penalty in preoccupation with that premium that only architects can evaluate. There is no way for an architect to withdraw from his responsibilities as a design professional in this regard."

THE PRIVATE DEVELOPER AS CLIENT

The following condensation of a section of the GSA report previously cited reveals some of the basic differences between the private and public client.

"When developers build commercial office buildings, financial conditions require them to minimize the cost of construction and to strive to earn rental income at the earliest possible moment. As a result, they propose extremely tight schedules to the contractor and the architect. Thereafter, they rely on the contractor to be the major force in adhering to the agreed-upon schedule. The contractor performs this task during design by constantly work-

CLIENTS: PUBLIC AND PRIVATE 75

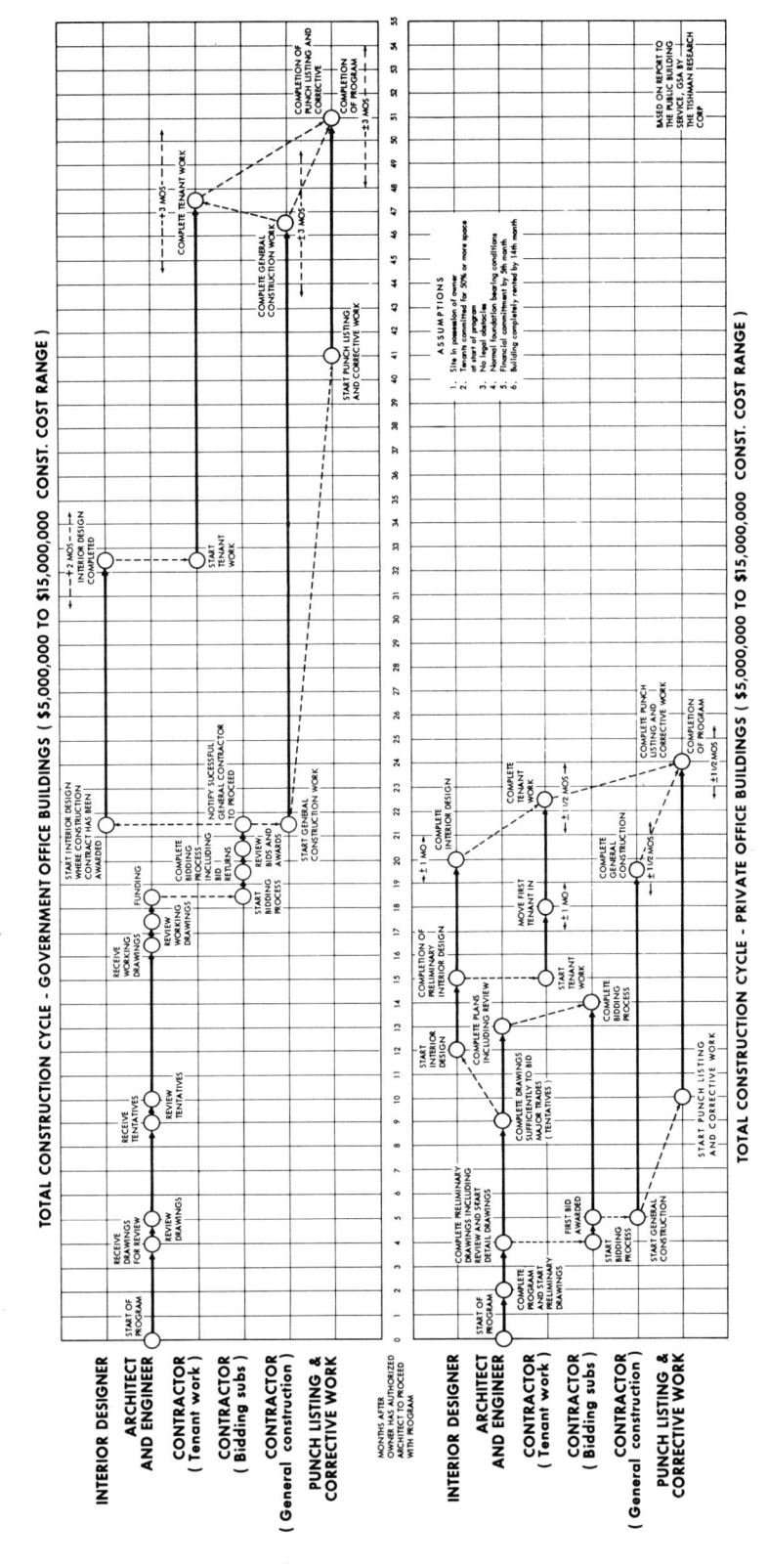

ing with the architect and providing expertise on construction techniques and market conditions. The contractor also establishes the construction schedule (using CPM where deemed appropriate) and assures compliance when he manages the construction of the building (if he acts as the general contractor or the construction manager). This organizational arrangement coupled with the motivations of the commercial marketplace produces office buildings more expeditiously than any other arrangement observed by the study group."

Phased design and construction is one of the major techniques used by developers and their contractors to compress the time needed to obtain new buildings. This is in contrast with the conventional government process (see chart, page 75) where the sequence of events has heretofore been consecutive. While phased construction increases the risk of a high incidence of changes during construction, developers have not found this to be a significant problem.

WHAT HAPPENS TO QUALITY OF THE BUILDING

Most of the contractors surveyed by the GSA study group pointed out that the key difficulty in today's construction market is determining the most cost-effective components of a building at any given time. It was their view that the continuing availability of new products and the wide fluctuations in cost and availability of construction labor made it very difficult to predict the best solution far in advance. In order to compensate for this difficulty, developers of commercial office buildings are using systems which provide the greatest possible flexibility. In many cases, this is done by the use of performance-type specifications or, at least, specifications which are substantially less detailed than in the past. In this regard, present-day specifications are tending to leave many more options open until the time of construction and more frequently to solicit bids on specified alternatives. These techniques are possible when the contractor (as construction manager) is working on the project throughout the design period, since he is aware of the intent of the broader specifications and is motivated by the arrangement to seek the best possible solution.

Although the general contractor frequently works with the architect during design, it appears that a number of the cost-reduction changes occur after bids have been obtained. When the specialty contractors submit their detailed bids on, for example, the mechanical and electrical systems, the AE and/or construction manager may find that an alternate product or technique is available at a lower cost than the material or techniques originally specified. A number of the contractors surveyed pointed out that this result was inevitable, *since the detailed expertise in these areas resides with the specialty subcontractors* rather than with the general contractor. It therefore appears that a significant way in which developers achieve cost reductions is by undertaking a substantial amount of cost-benefit analysis immediately after bids are in. It should be noted that this technique provides a developer (and his architect and construction manager) with a very effective method of making cost-benefit analyses of all components of the building, based on current prices and the latest available products.

The contractors indicated that this system did not necessarily degrade the quality of the building. In fact, several contractors mentioned extremely high-quality buildings which were done using these techniques. The key to controlling quality apparently lies in a firm definition by all parties—architect, engineer, contractor, developer—of the quality level desired, and willingness to maintain this level.

Commercial developers believe that they obtain lower costs using construction manager techniques than could be obtained through a sequential design, competitive bid, construction system. They retain the benefits of competition (from specialty contractors) on the bulk of the project with the added benefit of constant effort throughout the project to achieve the most cost-effective design. They believe that the old system of inviting competitive bids on a fixed design unnecessarily commits the owner to courses of action which may significantly increase the costs of the project and which cannot be altered without uneconomic redesign and loss of time. (In short, they commit themselves to increased owner-participation for profit.)

MANAGEMENT ABILITY OF DEVELOPER IS VITAL
The contractors surveyed by the GSA task force vigorously stated that decision-making capability by the developer (as project administrator) is a necessary element of the phased method of construction. The close coordination between the architectural design and the construction management functions provides a constant stream of alternate products and techniques which can be used. This necessitates a substantial number of expeditious decisions by the developer's project administrator if the schedule is to be met.

In all cases where the contractor (or other construction manager) is brought into the project at approximately the same time as the architect, the selection criteria must necessarily be based on his over-all ability rather than on price competition. Developers frequently seek a limited number of management proposals and select that contractor (or management firm) who has the most relevant background and offers the most attractive proposal as to methods which will be used to manage the job.

DEVELOPER-MANAGER-CONTRACTOR ARRANGEMENTS
Flexible business arrangements can be used by developers. The major ones in current use, according to the GSA report are as follows:

CLIENTS: PUBLIC AND PRIVATE

1. *Competitively Bid General Contract.* Occasionally developers have hired a contractor as a consultant during the design of a building and thereafter have put the construction out to competitive bidding. In such cases, if the consultant-contractor was not the low bidder, he did not receive the award. Most of the contractors interviewed stated that they were willing to work under such an arrangement but that it reduces their over-all effectiveness. The difficulty with this arrangement is that the achievement of the best building for the lowest cost requires a continual effort from early in design through construction, and this continuity is broken if competition is injected midway into the process.

2. *Guaranteed Maximum Price.* The most common practice seems to be for the developer to agree to a guaranteed maximum price when the architect's concepts are sufficiently well-defined to provide a firm statement of the design of the building and the components which will be used. Generally, this guaranteed maximum price is at or below the project budget. If it is not, the developer may insist on extensive work by the architect and the contractor to reduce costs. Under this business arrangement, the contractor generally receives a share of cost savings below the guaranteed maximum in the range of 10 to 50 per cent. Several contractors noted that there had been significant cost savings under some of these arrangements, with developers finally paying up to 7 or 8 per cent less than the guaranteed maximum price. In this situation, the contractor, of course, is free to bargain with subcontractors and performs the work in the same manner that he would under a fixed-price general contract.

3. *Construction Management for a Fee.* In some instances the contractor tends to do very little work with his own forces, i.e., generally only housekeeping jobs at the site. Thus, all major work is bought in the name of the developer from firms that would normally be subcontractors, with the contractor acting primarily as a manager, purchasing agent, and supervisor of construction. In these cases, the contractors noted that they were unusually free to represent the interests of the developer in an unbiased fashion (once they had successfully negotiated the shift from entrepreneurial to professional management service).

6 | CONTRACTS AND PROPOSALS

Contracts and proposals for construction management, despite obvious differences in scope and legal consequence, are similar in that each provides a basic checklist of services that define the construction manager's role in explicit terms. The proposal may have formal requirements, as described for PBS in Chapter 5, but in general is based on what the professional CM regards as the services actually required for a given project. The contract is the sifted remainder of those services to which the owner agrees. As both owners and professionals mature in this arena, the possibility of standard forms increases. While the inevitable imprint of special interests emerges in those forms (GSA, AIA, AGC, etc.) all are subject to a central professional theme. A summary of items that might be considered would include (but not be limited to) the following from a real commission:

1) A general statement based on client's needs in handling several design firms in addition to the firm offering professional management

CONTRACTS AND PROPOSALS

services. It is condensed and made anonymous to avoid any implication that it is a pattern to be followed in detail.

"In response to a notification of commission dated ___, relating to Project Blank, the Construction Management Firm (CMF) proposes to perform the general management services as set forth in Section I below; and shall furnish specific services as set forth in Sections II through XV.

Section I—General:

a) To establish and implement a comprehensive management program including all direction, procedures, coordination, administration, review, expediting, and counseling, required to assist the client and his consultants in accomplishing the Project in a timely, economical, and acceptable manner.

b) To furnish and administer a number of management systems or programs, including cost control, scheduling, management information, public and community relations, project communications, contracting and procurement, and project accounting; and to provide all services required for their operation.

c) To provide professional and technical support for the project's construction consultation and management functions as required, including but not limited to economic surveys, contract counseling, disputes arbitration, and community relations counseling.

d) To implement a program of *construction consultation* review and coordination of the design development activities and to staff a project office to accomplish this program.

e) To implement a program of *construction management,* inspection, coordination, and expediting, for all project construction activity, and to staff a project office to accomplish this program.

f) To provide and supervise an administrative staff for the project office, including all required administrative support for designated representatives of the Owners."

Sections II through XV would then detail personnel, systems, procedures, etc.

2) Specific definitions of each service should be spelled out, and the executive personnel responsible for their performance may be named. Many of the services listed in Chapter 3 might be included in these specifics, but would be expanded and defined to accommodate special resources of the CM firm, such as proprietary computer programs or CPM specialties. While each of these services is separately identified, some effort should be made to relate them as components of a single over-all management process.

Ideally, they should be marshalled as interrelated groups of service, like modules, contributing to total unity of the project from conception through decision and design to delivery. The reason for this seemingly extra attention to relationships is the fact that they have a great deal to do with the clarity and effectiveness of the professional contract. The modular separation of pre-bid and post-bid services is one of the obvious modes of marshalling, but within those two categories there are sub-sets of services that can be grouped for improved understanding and definition of their purposes.

The specific number of estimates, their level of detail and the point in time at which they are to be made should be itemized.

3) Staffing of the management function should be covered in specific terms. Not only the numbers of people to be mustered, but their specific duties and the names of their supervisors may reinforce the CM's approaches to discussions of compensation.

4) Subcontracting of certain items among the services proposed should be reviewed as a possibility and either made part of the agreement or specifically excluded. For example:

"Computerized processing of the CPM control shall be performed by XYZ Central Services at (specified) intervals and reimbursed as (whatever terms are reasonable in consideration of the fee structure)."

Or: "None of these services shall be subcontracted to other consultants without written consent of the Owner."

5) Responsibilities of the various parties involved should be spelled out in as much detail as possible. While there are many gray areas still untested in the courts, the experience of conventional professional practice and construction contracting provides adequate guidelines. Responsibilities of the management firm toward owners, other professionals and contractors should follow along the well established lines of traditional professional relationships. The legal implications of difference between foremanship (i.e., specific direction of the work) and field observation or review (i.e., surveillance and interpretation of the intent of construction documents) have already been stressed here and in many other publications. The wording of contracts should sustain awareness of these implications. In somewhat simplistic terms, for example, the professional's field personnel "don't tell the carpenter where, when or how to drive his nails. They do tell his boss when he is driving them contrary to the intent of design or at a pace incompatible with contracted schedule."

The limits of time within which the CM bears responsibility for completion should also be clearly stated. An experienced construction manager knows how long it takes to build a building, and he commits himself professionally to that knowledge; but he does not know what unforeseeable conditions, physical, political or financial, may impose delays over which he has no control. Those delays can cost him money, even though the scope of the work is not enlarged, so he should stipulate his compensation in the event of such delays.

It should be borne in mind that liability in the area of construction management is a whole new issue. Those gray areas mentioned above can turn black or white on the ability of the courts to understand the commitments of the parties and the meanings of words (like supervision) in the contract. The contract should say who is responsible for what. For example, architects, engineers, contractors, managers and others all make estimates. None can be construed, by language of the contract, to be irresponsible.

6) Insurance coverage is also related to liability exposures. The kind and amount of insurance policies should be stated—both those which are particular to the project and those which are carried for professional liability coverage. For example, in addition to workmen's compensation, public liability and property damage insurance, a recent New Jersey contract stipulated that:

> "The Construction Management Consultant shall provide and pay for insurance for professional liability. The *certificate of insurance* shall be filed with the Director at the time of signing of the Construction Management contract agreement. The Construction Management professional liability policy shall include the limit of liability per claim and the aggregate amount payable. Such insurance shall be equal in amount to the errors and omissions insurance carried by the architects administering for the project."

Professionals should bear in mind that their errors and omissions insurance, although it may cover an expansion of professional services during the construction phase, does not cover any extension of those services beyond professional bounds. The same professional bounds already defined in AIA documents obtain throughout professional construction management. The area of construction methods, means and techniques is uninsurable by any professional liability policy. The architect or engineer who practices construction management may find himself tempted into at least two sensitive areas where his liability coverage may be inoperative. First is the area of safety provisions on the job. While he may contract to observe safety conditions, he should be sure that his contract does not commit him to direct responsibility for such provisions as barriers or scaffolds. These are the contractor's responsibility. The professional can report safety violations, but he should not commit himself to physical participation in their correction.

A second sensitive area has to do with schedules of work. Where sur-

CONTRACTS AND PROPOSALS

veillance of schedules is part of the professional construction management service, there appears to be coverage available, but the limits of that coverage should be carefully checked with the insurance carrier.

Just as architects and engineers cannot get coverage for construction methods and techniques, contractors in the CM role who increase their presence during design phases cannot be insured against errors and omissions in plans and specifications. Even though the contractor works on a fee basis, this kind of professional liability insurance is written only for architects and engineers in private practice.

All of this pertains also to the contract for general requirements on the site of a multiple contract job. The general requirements are, in fact, performed under a construction contract, and any professional who chooses to handle that contract himself should check with his carrier to ascertain the extent of his professional coverage. In any event, that coverage will not protect him against liability for construction methods and techniques used under the general requirements contract.

7) Responsibility for general requirements of contractors in the field should be detailed, including such items as the provision of field offices, the location of central records, the engineering and installation of temporary heating facilities and sanitary facilities, safety measures, etc. The detail of this cannot be overdone, since general requirements are so variously interpreted from one job to another.

8) Conventional and/or repetitive sections, such as might be derived from well-known documents of the AIA and contractor organizations should be judiciously selected. These are familiar as background to contracting procedures and can facilitate understanding.

9) Specifics of the fees for services outlined should be written in complete detail, including cutoff dates for the management services. If there is a possibility that the project might be extended in time beyond the limits foreseen in the negotiating period, a cost to the management firm of maintaining surveillance of the project can be considerable even though the actual scope of the job may not be substantially increased.

10) Scope of the project should be carefully spelled out as to size, number of buildings, total square feet, dollar value and target completion date realistically estimated.

THE PROTOTYPE CONTRACT

The foregoing outline of principles is applied with remarkable consistency to a great deal of work that has been done since 1971 in developing prototype contracts for construction management. The contract published in April 1975 by GSA, mentioned in Chapter 5, occupies some 50 pages in the GSA report. It reflects all the bureaucratic and legal restrictions with which that Agency must deal in providing this service on behalf of the Federal Government and the U.S. taxpayer. It is, therefore, a formidable and in fact cumbersome document, but it contains a body of principle that is common to many such contracts for professional construction management. An index of the sixty clauses in the document is shown below. The full text can be found in the publication, "The GSA System for Construction Management," available from the GSA Public Buildings Service, 18th & F Streets, N.W., Washington, D.C. 20405.

Those clauses in the contract that may stir some curiosity if not dismay on the part of architects and engineers have to do with the elements common to design and construction. Clause 5, for example, deals with the management plan for design and construction and stipulates that the CM shall develop a plan (including the schedule) for all three phases: design, overlap (a period beginning with the letting of the first bid in phases construction) and construction of the project. The management plan for the design phase is to be submitted within 30 days after award of the CM contract. Those elements of the management plan that apply to design schedule will have to be reconciled with the A-E firm involved.

Clause 6, on design development and review, enjoins the CM to familiarize himself thoroughly with evolving architectural and engineering plans

---

Basic operating requirements for the construction manager

The lump sum contract is negotiated as a contract for construction management services pursuant to Sections 302 (c) (10) and 307 of the Federal Property and Administrative Services Act of 1949, as amended. A lump sum price, ranging normally from 2 to 4 per cent of the estimated construction cost, is agreed upon as total compensation for the contract services. Reimbursement for the actual costs of certain designated services and general condition items is also provided. An effort is made to award the CM contract prior to the A-E contract. Following is an index of clauses in the CM contract:

1. Project
2. Definitions
3. General
4. Construction management control system
5. Management plan for design and construction
6. Design development and review
7. Long lead procurement
8. Separate contracts planning
9. Interfacing
10. Job-site facilities
11. Weather protection
12. Solicitation of bids
13. Market analysis and stimulation of bidder interest
14. Managing and inspecting construction
15. Monitoring submittals
16. Subcontractor or material vendor recommendations
17. Comprehensive safety program
18. Labor relations
19. Construction contract changes
20. Value management
21. Claims
22. Meetings and conferences
23. Home office support for job-site staff
24. Reimbursable services
25. General condition items
26. Reimbursable costs
27. Lump sum contract price
28. Payment
29. Staff (nonreimbursable)
30. Subcontracting
31. Federal, State and local taxes
32. Time for completion
33. Suspension of work
34. Changes
35. Pricing of adjustments
36. Disputes
37. Payment of interest on CM's claims
38. Termination
39. Partial termination for untimely performance
40. Covenant against contingent fees
41. Officials not to benefit
42. Convict labor
43. Prohibition against bidding
44. Utilization of small business concerns
45. Equal opportunity
46. Certification of nonsegregated facilities
47. Utilization of minority business enterprises
48. Minority enterprises subcontracting program
49. Listing of employment openings
50. Employment of the handicapped
51. Liability for damage
52. Accident prevention for general conditions work
53. Performance and payment bonds
54. Labor standards
55. Davis-Bacon wage rate decision
56. Home-town or imposed plan—minority hiring
57. Buy American
58. Examination of records
59. Cost accounting standards
60. Energy conservation and environmental protection.

CONTRACTS AND PROPOSALS

and specifications and "make recommendations with respect to the site, foundations, selection of systems and materials and cost-reducing alternatives." It is not implied that these recommendations usurp design prerogatives or preempt the specifying role of architects and engineers. On the other hand, the clause contains the enjoinder that: "He (the CM) shall submit to the Government such comments as may be appropriate concerning construction feasibility and practicality. He shall call to the Government's attention any apparent defects in the design."

The CM is also supposed to review each bid package as the A-E completes it and promptly submit to the Contracting Officer a written report "covering action taken by the A-E with respect to suggestions or recommendations previously submitted . . ." It is not hard to envision friction points in some of these provisions.

On balance, one can hope for the lubrication of good will and an instinct for survival at these friction points. Some perspective may be gained from a comment under the heading "trends to the future" stating: "GSA is convinced that communication, cooperation, research, feedback, flexibility and receptivity on an industry-wide basis must be the watch-words if the construction industry is to have a productive future in a world faced with continuing energy and material scarcities. The construction industry's key role . . . makes these watch-words imperative."

One of the unique characters of the GSA contract is its insistence upon the use of a Computerized Management Control System (CMCS). This is a program for use with large computers, and successful applicants for GSA work must purchase the program from GSA (at cost for about $39). The publication describes the system as follows: The PBS-CMCS, made up of sophisticated modules for: 1) schedule, and progress control; 2) project cost control, and 3) project financial control, brings together, and presents in timely, organized formats, the many different items of information which are needed to effectively manage a project. The reports are structured horizontally by the three information types and vertically by management level on a "need-to-know" basis that is oriented toward the user. Such a system can provide:
• Information when it is needed through the use of automated data processing techniques;
• Formats that are flexible enough to reflect the unique management requirements of a particular project;
• Formats that are flexible enough to reflect the unique management require-summaries) reflect the most recent data developed in other parts of the system (i.e., recent schedule changes for their impact on cost escalation, change order requests, etc.);

CONTRACTS AND PROPOSALS

- Arrow diagram networks identifying and controlling all activities from the start of design to the completion of construction;
- Detailed printouts covering every aspect of the design-construct process;
- Schedules expediting purchase orders, shop drawings, and samples;
- Cost data organized by building systems for use as meaningful design parameters;
- Cost data organized by trades to conform with construction bid and change order reviews;
- Financial reports to control fund availability, requirements and commitments, and payments; and
- *Real* job status with an overall view of the project.

"The use of the PBS-CMCS is now mandatory on our projects. GSA will no longer permit substitution of other control systems."

AIA develops CM documents

The American Institute of Architects, in an effort of similar magnitude but perhaps less encumbered by regulations has issued a series of documents adapted for the presence of a professional construction manager within the normal process of design and delivery of buildings. The key document is B801 "Standard Form of Agreement Between Owner and Construction Manager." This was a result of more than two years of work by the Institute's Document Board, gathering information and review from practicing construction managers, architects, engineers, general contractors and federal agencies. The document was published in December 1973 and was followed by further adaptations and other AIA documents to take into account the effect of construction management on the whole process. These adaptations have been issued as A101/CM The Construction Management Edition of the Standard Form of Agreement Between Owner and Contractor; Document B141/CM, Standard Form of Agreement Between Owner and Architect; and Document A201/CM General Conditions of Contract for Construction. All this work is under constant review, but radical changes are unlikely, since the development of principles and definition of CM services proceeded with fair consistency with opening pages of this chapter, thus indicating that principles and practices have been substantially formulated for refined definition in B801.

AIA Document B801 in its entirety is only ten pages long, with the first four pages devoted to the usual statements of contracting parties and terms of compensation. Key Pages defining the services are reproduced on the following pages.

It should be noted that, as key documents such as A201 are revised in important ways, B801 and related CM documents will also be reviewed.

CONTRACTS AND PROPOSALS

> **TERMS AND CONDITIONS OF AGREEMENT BETWEEN OWNER AND CONSTRUCTION MANAGER**

ARTICLE 1

CONSTRUCTION MANAGER'S SERVICES

1.1 BASIC SERVICES

The Construction Manager's Basic Services consist of the two phases described below and any other services included in Article 13 as Basic Services.

DESIGN PHASE

1.1.1 *Consultation During Project Development:* Review conceptual designs during development. Advise on site use and improvements, selection of materials, building systems and equipment. Provide recommendations on relative construction feasibility, availability of materials and labor, time requirements for installation and construction, and factors related to cost including costs of alternative designs or materials, preliminary budgets, and possible economies.

1.1.2 *Scheduling:* Provide and periodically update a Project time schedule that coordinates and integrates the Architect's services with construction schedules.

1.1.3 *Project Budget:* Prepare a Project budget for the Owner's approval as soon as major Project requirements have been identified and update periodically. Prepare an estimate of construction cost based on a quantity survey of Drawings and Specifications at the end of the Schematic Design Phase for approval by the Owner. Update and refine this estimate for Owner's approval as the development of the Drawings and Specifications proceeds, and advise the Owner and the Architect if it appears that the Project budget will not be met and make recommendations for corrective action.

1.1.4 *Coordination of Contract Documents:* Review the Drawings and Specifications as they are being prepared, recommending alternative solutions whenever design details affect construction feasibility or schedules.

1.1.4.1 Verify that the requirements and assignment of responsibilities for safety precautions and programs, temporary Project facilities and for equipment, materials and services for common use of Contractors are included in the proposed Contract Documents.

1.1.4.2 Advise on the method to be used for selecting Contractors and awarding contracts. If separate contracts are to be awarded, review the Drawings and Specifications to (1) ascertain if areas of jurisdiction overlap, (2) verify that all Work has been included, and (3) allow for phased construction.

1.1.4.3 Investigate and recommend a schedule for purchase by the Owner of all materials and equipment requiring long lead time procurement, and coordinate the schedule with the early preparation of Contract Documents by the Architect. Expedite and coordinate delivery of these purchases.

1.1.5 *Labor:* Provide an analysis of the types and quantity of labor required for the Project and review the availability of appropriate categories of labor required for critical phases.

1.1.5.1 Determine applicable requirements for equal employment opportunity programs for inclusion in the proposed Contract Documents.

1.1.6 *Bidding:* Prepare pre-qualification criteria for bidders and develop Contractor interest in the Project. Establish bidding schedules and conduct pre-bid conferences to familiarize bidders with the bidding documents and management techniques and with any special systems, materials or methods.

1.1.6.1 Receive bids, prepare bid analyses and make recommendations to the Owner for award of contracts or rejection of bids.

1.1.7 *Contract Awards:* Conduct pre-award conferences with successful bidders. Assist the Owner in preparing Construction Contracts and advise the Owner on the acceptability of Subcontractors and material suppliers proposed by Contractors.

CONSTRUCTION PHASE

The Construction Phase will commence with the award of the first Construction Contract or purchase order and will terminate 30 days after the final Certificate for Payment is issued by the Architect.

1.1.8 *Project Control:* Coordinate the Work of the Contractors with the activities and responsibilities of the Owner and Architect to complete the Project in accordance with the Owner's objectives on cost, time and quality. Provide sufficient personnel at the Project site with authority to achieve these objectives.

1.1.8.1 Schedule and conduct pre-construction and progress meetings at which Contractors, Owner, Architect and Construction Manager can discuss jointly such matters as procedures, progress, problems and scheduling.

1.1.8.2 Provide a detailed schedule for the operations of Contractors on the Project, including realistic activity sequences and durations, allocation of labor and materials, processing of shop drawings and samples, and delivery of products requiring long lead time procurement; include the Owner's occupancy requirements showing portions of the Project having occupancy priority.

1.1.8.3 Provide regular monitoring of the schedule as construction progresses. Identify potential variances between scheduled and probable completion dates. Review schedule for Work not started or incomplete and recommend to the Owner and Contractor adjustments in the schedule to meet the probable completion date. Provide summary reports of each monitoring, and document all changes in schedule.

1.1.8.4 Recommend courses of action to the Owner when requirements of a contract are not being fulfilled.

AIA DOCUMENT B801 • OWNER-CONSTRUCTION MANAGER AGREEMENT • DECEMBER 1973 EDITION • AIA®
© 1973 • THE AMERICAN INSTITUTE OF ARCHITECTS, 1735 NEW YORK AVE., N.W., WASHINGTON, D. C. 20006

CONTRACTS AND PROPOSALS

1.1.9 *Cost Control:* Revise and refine the approved estimate of construction cost, incorporate approved changes as they occur, and develop cash flow reports and forecasts as needed.

1.1.9.1 Provide regular monitoring of the approved estimate of construction cost, showing actual costs for activities in process and estimates for uncompleted tasks. Identify variances between actual and budgeted or estimated costs, and advise the Owner and Architect whenever projected costs exceed budgets or estimates.

1.1.9.2 Arrange for the maintenance of cost accounting records on authorized Work performed under unit costs, actual costs for labor and materials, or other bases requiring accounting records.

1.1.9.3 Develop and implement a system for review and processing of Change Orders.

1.1.9.4 Recommend necessary or desirable changes to the Owner and the Architect, review requests for changes, submit recommendations to the Owner and the Architect, and assist in negotiating Change Orders.

1.1.9.5 Develop and implement a procedure for the review and processing of applications by Contractors for progress and final payments. Make recommendations to the Architect for certification to the Owner for payment.

1.1.10 *Permits and Fees:* Assist in obtaining all building permits and special permits for permanent improvements, excluding permits for inspection or temporary facilities required to be obtained directly by the various Contractors. Verify that the Owner has paid all applicable fees and assessments for permanent facilities. Assist in obtaining approvals from all the authorities having jurisdiction.

1.1.11 *Owner's Consultants:* If required, assist the Owner in selecting and retaining professional services of a surveyor, special consultants and testing laboratories. Coordinate these services.

1.1.12 *Inspection:* Inspect the work of Contractors to assure that the Work is being performed in accordance with the requirements of the Contract Documents. Endeavor to guard the Owner against defects and deficiencies in the Work. Require any Contractor to stop Work or any portion thereof, and require special inspection or testing of any Work not in accordance with the provisions of the Contract Documents whether or not such Work be then fabricated, installed or completed. Reject Work which does not conform to the requirements of the Contract Documents.

1.1.12.1 The Construction Manager shall not be responsible for construction means, methods, techniques, sequences and procedures employed by Contractors in performance of their contract, and he shall not be responsible for the failure of any Contractors to carry out the Work in accordance with the Contract Documents.

1.1.13 *Contract Performance:* Consult with the Architect and the Owner if any Contractor requests interpretations of the meaning and intent of the Drawings and Specifications, and assist in the resolution of any questions which may arise.

1.1.14 *Shop Drawings and Samples:* In collaboration with the Architect, establish and implement procedures for expediting the processing and approval of shop drawings and samples.

1.1.15 *Reports and Records:* Record the progress of the Project. Submit written progress reports to the Owner and the Architect including information on the Contractors and Work, the percentage of completion and the number and amounts of Change Orders. Keep a daily log available to the Owner and the Architect.

1.1.15.1 Maintain at the Project site, on a current basis: records of all Contracts; shop drawings; samples; purchases; materials; equipment; applicable handbooks; federal, commercial and technical standards and specifications; maintenance and operating manuals and instructions; and any other related documents and revisions which arise out of the Contract or the Work. Obtain data from Contractors and maintain a current set of record drawings, specifications and operating manuals. At the completion of the Project, deliver all such records to the Owner.

1.1.16 *Owner-Purchased Items:* Accept delivery and arrange storage, protection and security for all Owner-purchased materials, systems and equipment which are a part of the Work until such items are turned over to the Contractors.

1.1.17 *Substantial Completion:* Upon the Contractors' determination of Substantial Completion of the Work or designated portions thereof, prepare for the Architect a list of incomplete or unsatisfactory items and a schedule for their completion. After the Architect certifies the Date of Substantial Completion, supervise the correction and completion of Work.

1.1.18 *Start-Up:* With the Owner's maintenance personnel, direct the checkout of utilities, operational systems and equipment for readiness and assist in their initial start-up and testing.

1.1.19 *Final Completion:* Determine final completion and provide written notice to the Owner and Architect that the Work is ready for final inspection. Secure and transmit to the Architect required guarantees, affidavits, releases, bonds and waivers. Turn over to the Owner all keys, manuals, record drawings and maintenance stocks.

1.2 ADDITIONAL SERVICES

The following Additional Services shall be performed upon authorization in writing from the Owner and shall be paid for as hereinbefore provided.

1.2.1 Services related to investigation, appraisals or valuations of existing conditions, facilities or equipment, or verifying the accuracy of existing drawings or other Owner-furnished information.

1.2.2 Services related to Owner-furnished equipment, furniture and furnishings which are not a part of the Work.

1.2.3 Services for tenant or rental spaces.

1.2.4 Services related to construction performed by the Owner.

1.2.5 Consultation on replacement of Work damaged by

fire or other cause during construction, and furnishing services for the replacement of such Work.

1.2.6 Services made necessary by the default of a Contractor.

1.2.7 Preparing to serve or serving as an expert witness in connection with any public hearing, arbitration proceeding, or legal proceeding.

1.2.8 Finding housing for construction labor, and defining requirements for establishment and maintenance of base camps.

1.2.9 Obtaining or training maintenance personnel or negotiating maintenance service contracts.

1.2.10 Services related to Work items required by the Conditions of the Contract and the Specifications which are not provided by Contractors.

1.2.11 Inspections of and services related to the Project after completion of the services under this Agreement.

1.2.12 Providing any other service not otherwise included in this Agreement.

ARTICLE 2

THE OWNER'S RESPONSIBILITIES

2.1 The Owner shall provide full information regarding his requirements for the Project.

2.2 The Owner shall designate a representative who shall be fully acquainted with the scope of the Work, and has authority to render decisions promptly and furnish information expeditiously.

2.3 The Owner shall retain an Architect for design and to prepare construction documents for the Project. The Architect's services, duties and responsibilities are described in the Agreement between the Owner and the Architect, pertinent parts of which will be furnished to the Construction Manager and will not be modified without written notification to him.

2.4 The Owner shall furnish such legal, accounting and insurance counselling services as may be necessary for the Project, and such auditing services as he may require to ascertain how or for what purposes the Contractors have used the moneys paid to them under the Construction Contracts.

2.5 The Owner shall furnish the Construction Manager with a sufficient quantity of construction documents.

2.6 If the Owner becomes aware of any fault or defect in the Project or nonconformance with the Contract Documents, he shall give prompt written notice thereof to the Construction Manager.

2.7 The services, information, surveys and reports required by Paragraphs 2.3 through 2.5 inclusive shall be furnished at the Owner's expense, and the Construction Manager shall be entitled to rely upon the accuracy and completeness thereof.

ARTICLE 3

CONSTRUCTION COST

3.1 If the Construction Cost is to be used as the basis for determining the Construction Manager's compensation for Basic Services, it shall be the cost of all Work, including work items in the Conditions of the Contract and the Specifications and shall be determined as follows:

3.1.1 For completed construction, the total construction cost of all such Work;

3.1.2 For Work not constructed, (1) the sum of the lowest bona fide bids received from qualified bidders for any or all of such Work or (2) if the Work is not bid, the sum of the bona fide negotiated proposals submitted for any or all of such Work; or

3.1.3 For Work for which no such bids or proposals are received, the Construction Cost contained in the Construction Manager's latest Project construction budget approved by the Owner.

3.2 Construction Cost shall not include the compensation of the Construction Manager (except for costs of Work items in the Conditions of the Contract and in the Specifications), the Architect and consultants, the cost of the land, rights-of-way, or other costs which are the responsibility of the Owner as provided in Paragraphs 2.3 through 2.5 inclusive.

3.3 The cost of labor, materials and equipment furnished by the Owner shall be included in the Construction Cost at current market rates, including a reasonable allowance for overhead and profit.

3.4 Cost estimates prepared by the Construction Manager represent his best judgment as a professional familiar with the construction industry. It is recognized, however, that neither the Construction Manager nor the Owner has any control over the cost of labor, materials or equipment, over Contractors' methods of determining bid prices, or other competitive bidding or market conditions.

3.5 No fixed limit of Construction Cost shall be deemed to have been established unless it is in writing and signed by the parties hereto. When a fixed limit of Construction Cost is established in writing as a condition of this Agreement, the Construction Manager shall advise what materials, equipment, component systems and types of construction should be included in the Contract Documents, and shall suggest reasonable adjustments in the scope of the Project to bring it within the fixed limit.

3.5.1. If responsive bids are not received as scheduled, any fixed limit of Construction Cost established as a condition of this Agreement shall be adjusted to reflect any change in the general level of prices occurring between the originally scheduled date and the date on which bids are received.

3.5.2 When the fixed limit of Construction Cost is exceeded, the Owner shall (1) give written approval of an increase in such fixed limit, (2) authorize rebidding within a reasonable time, or (3) cooperate in revising the scope and quality of the Work as required to reduce the Construction Cost. In the case of (3) the Construction Manager, without additional compensation, shall cooperate with the Architect as necessary to bring the Construction Cost within the fixed limit.

ARTICLE 4

DIRECT PERSONNEL EXPENSE

Direct Personnel Expense is defined as the salaries of professional, technical and clerical employees engaged on the Project by the Construction Manager, and the cost of their mandatory and customary benefits such as statutory employee benefits, insurance, sick leave, holidays, vacations, pensions and similar benefits.

ARTICLE 5

REIMBURSABLE EXPENSES

5.1 Reimbursable Expenses are in addition to the compensation for Basic and Additional Services and include actual expenditures made by the Construction Manager, his employees, or his professional consultants in the interest of the Project:

5.1.1 Long distance calls and telegrams, and fees paid for securing approval of authorities having jurisdiction over the Project.

5.1.2 Handling, shipping, mailing and reproduction of Project related materials.

5.1.3 Transportation and living when traveling in connection with the Project, relocation costs, and overtime work requiring higher than regular rates if authorized in advance by the Owner.

5.1.4 Electronic data processing service and rental of electronic data processing equipment when used in connection with Additional Services.

5.1.5 Premiums for insurance required in Article 10.

5.1.6 Providing construction support activities such as Work items included in the Conditions of the Contract and in the Specifications unless they are provided by the Contractors.

ARTICLE 6

PAYMENTS TO THE CONSTRUCTION MANAGER

6.1 Payments shall be made monthly upon presentation of the Construction Manager's statement of services as follows:

6.1.1 An initial payment as set forth in Paragraph IIB is the minimum payment under this Agreement.

6.1.2 When compensation is computed as described in Paragraphs IIA1a, IIA3, or IIA4, subsequent payments for Basic Services shall be made in proportion to services performed. The compensation at the completion of each Phase shall equal the following percentages of the total compensation for Basic Services:

    Design Phase 20%
    Construction Phase 100%

6.1.3 Payments for Reimbursable Expenses shall be made upon presentation of the Construction Manager's statement.

6.2 No deductions shall be made from the Construction Manager's compensation on account of penalty, liquidated damages, or other sums withheld from payments to Contractors.

6.3 If the Project is suspended for more than three months or abandoned in whole or in part, the Construction Manager shall be paid his compensation for services performed prior to receipt of written notice from the Owner of such suspension or abandonment, together with Reimbursable Expenses then due, and all termination expenses as defined in Paragraph 7.2 resulting from such suspension or abandonment. If the Project is resumed after being suspended for more than three months, the Construction Manager's compensation shall be subject to renegotiation.

6.4 If construction of the Project has started and is delayed by reason of strikes, or other circumstance not due to the fault of the Construction Manager, the Owner shall reimburse the Construction Manager for the costs of his Project-site staff as provided for by this Agreement. The Construction Manager shall reduce the size of his Project-site staff after a 60-day delay, or sooner if feasible, for the remainder of the delay period as directed by the Owner and, during the period, the Owner shall reimburse the Construction Manager for the direct personnel expense of such staff plus any relocation costs. Upon the termination of the delay, the Construction Manager shall restore his Project-site staff to its former size, subject to the approval of the Owner.

6.5 If the Project time schedule established in Subparagraph 1.1.2 is exceeded by more than thirty days through no fault of the Construction Manager, compensation for Basic Services performed by Principals, employees and professional consultants required beyond the thirtieth day to complete the services under this Agreement shall be as set forth in Paragraph IIC.

6.6 Payments due the Construction Manager which are unpaid for more than 60 days from date of billing shall bear interest at the legal rate of interest applicable at the construction site.

ARTICLE 7

TERMINATION OF AGREEMENT

7.1 This Agreement may be terminated by either party upon seven days' written notice should the other party fail substantially to perform in accordance with its terms through no fault of the party initiating termination. In the event of termination due to the fault of others than the Construction Manager, the Construction Manager shall be paid his compensation plus Reimbursable Expenses for services performed to termination date and all termination expenses.

7.2 Termination expenses are defined as Reimbursable Expenses directly attributable to termination, plus an amount computed as a percentage of the total compensation earned to the time of termination, as follows:

- 20 percent if termination occurs during the Design Phase; or
- 10 percent if termination occurs during the Construction Phase.

ARTICLE 8

SUCCESSORS AND ASSIGNS

The Owner and the Construction Manager each binds himself, his partners, successors, assigns and legal representatives to the other party to this Agreement and to the partners, successors, assigns and legal representatives of such other party with respect to all covenants of this Agreement. Neither the Owner nor the Construction Manager shall assign, sublet or transfer his interest in this Agreement without the written consent of the other.

ARTICLE 9

ARBITRATION

9.1 All claims, disputes and other matters in question between the parties to this Agreement, arising out of, or relating to this Agreement or the breach thereof, shall be decided by arbitration in accordance with the Construction Industry Arbitration Rules of the American Arbitration Association then obtaining unless the parties mutually agree otherwise. No arbitration, arising out of, or relating to this Agreement, shall include, by consolidation, joinder or in any other manner, any additional party not a party to this Agreement except by written consent containing a specific reference to this Agreement and signed by all the parties hereto. Any consent to arbitration involving an additional party or parties shall not constitute consent to arbitration of any dispute not described therein or with any party not named or described therein. This Agreement to arbitrate and any agreement to arbitrate with an additional party or parties duly consented to by the parties hereto shall be specifically enforceable under the prevailing arbitration law.

9.2 Notice of the demand for arbitration shall be filed in writing with the other party to this Agreement and with the American Arbitration Association. The demand shall be made within a reasonable time after the claim, dispute or other matter in question has arisen. In no event shall the demand for arbitration be made after the date when institution of legal or equitable proceedings based on such claim, dispute or other matter in question would be barred by the applicable statute of limitations.

9.3 The award rendered by the arbitrators shall be final, and judgment may be entered upon it in accordance with applicable law in any court having jurisdiction thereof.

ARTICLE 10

INSURANCE

The Construction Manager shall purchase and maintain insurance to protect himself from claims under workmen's compensation acts; claims for damages because of bodily injury including personal injury, sickness or disease, or death of any of his employees or of any person other than his employees; and from claims for damages because of injury to or destruction of tangible property including loss of use resulting therefrom; and from claims arising out of the performance of professional services caused by any errors, omissions or negligent acts for which he is legally liable.

ARTICLE 11

EXTENT OF AGREEMENT

11.1 This Agreement represents the entire and integrated agreement between the Owner and the Construction Manager and supersedes all prior negotiations, representations or agreements, either written or oral. This Agreement shall not be superseded by provisions of contracts for construction and may be amended only by written instrument signed by both Owner and Construction Manager.

11.2 Nothing contained herein shall be deemed to create any contractual relationship between the Construction Manager and the Architect or any of the Contractors, Subcontractors or material suppliers on the Project; nor shall anything contained herein be deemed to give any third party any claim or right of action against the Owner or the Construction Manager which does not otherwise exist without regard to this Agreement.

ARTICLE 12

GOVERNING LAW

Unless otherwise specified, this Agreement shall be governed by the law in effect at the location of the Project.

CONTRACTS AND PROPOSALS

PRIVATE INDUSTRY AGREEMENTS

Among private consultant firms, development of the prototype contract has been less circumscribed by either bureaucratic manipulations or the striving of committees for perfect accord with the special interests of institutional or association efforts. Nevertheless, most of the private agreements bear remarkable similarity in format and professional integrity to those developed by group processes, either governmental or institutional. A case in point is the agreement for construction management services between owner and construction manager developed by CM Associates, a firm headed by architect Charles Thomsen, independently affiliated with Caudill Rowlett Scott. Consistencies and some differences are apparent in the following terms of this contract.

```
ARTICLE I
BASIC SERVICES
```

The basic services of CM are the management of operations, costs, and agreements.

A   OPERATIONS

1   <u>Planning</u>: Appoint a project manager. Initiate a project manual which will summarize and track the essential operations, costs, and agreements associated with the project for the review of the owner and architect.

Conduct an owner/architect orientation meeting to establish project goals, a project strategy, procedures, responsibilities, and communications.

Establish a project directory containing names, addresses, telephone numbers, and functions of key individuals and companies connected with the project.

Continually review plans and specifications as they are being developed; advise on site use and improvements, construction feasibility, availability and cost of materials, labor, and building systems; advise on general and special conditions to the specifications to facilitate construction management procedures.

2   <u>Scheduling</u>: Provide an initial master schedule showing duration, responsibility, and precedence for major design, procurement, and construction activities; establish the overall duration of the project and identify those activities that are most critical; update the schedule and expand the level of detail as the project progresses.

Advise on contract provisions for controlling construction schedules; prepare schedules for inclusion in the bid documents for controlling duration and sequencing of each contractor's work.

CONTRACTS AND PROPOSALS

Work with each contractor to develop detailed operating schedules for his share of the work; monitor, update, and report on this schedule during the construction period.

3   Control: Hold regular meetings attended by the owner, architect, and contractors to coordinate the progress of the work; record and distribute minutes and decisions; keep all members of the team informed verbally and by means of monthly reports.

Prepare a contractors manual to instruct contractors on procedures for control of submittals, transmittals, field orders, change orders, directives, approvals, on-site communications, inspections, and requests for payments. Maintain a daily log.

Establish and coordinate an on-site construction management organization staffed as the owner and CM consider necessary; provide all facilities and equipment necessary to efficiently coordinate the construction work; clearly define roles of authority and responsibility of the field team.

Recommend a safety program to the owner and coordinate safety and security functions at the site. (The performance of this service by CM does not relieve the contractors of their responsibilities for the safety of persons and property and compliance with all federal, state, and local statutes, rules, regulations, and orders applicable to the conduct of the work; nor does it imply that CM assumes responsibility for the compliance thereof.)

Coordinate the check-out for operation and readiness of utilities, systems, and equipment and assist in the project testing and start-up programs.

B   COSTS

1   Budgeting: Assist the owner in providing an overall project budget, including construction costs, fees, owner's costs, contingencies, reserves, on-site overhead, and general conditions costs, which will be approved in writing by the owner and agreed to in writing by the architect.

Analyze overall project strategy and prepare recommendations to the owner for the accomplishment of general conditions construction; prepare budget for general conditions construction for owner's approval.

2   Value Engineering: Provide building systems cost data to owner and architect prior to design and analyze and report on the cost of alternative building systems and materials as design progresses.

3   Estimating: Periodically provide updated estimates and reports to the owner and architect and notify them if the project varies from the budget or if market fluctuations jeopardize the possibility of constructing the project within the budget.

4   Procurement: Review bid documents for clarity and advise the architect on procedures which will facilitate bid preparation. Establish a bidder's list; establish and evaluate qualifications, develop communications, hold or attend prebid conferences, and promote interest among potential contractors; negotiate and/or receive bids in behalf of the owner; analyze and advise the owner on the award of contracts; conduct preconstruction conferences with successful contractors; compare bid or negotiated proposals to estimates and

analyze the effect of actual bid prices on total project budget; review costs with bidders and negotiate economies if appropriate.

5   Project Accounting: Establish and periodically produce a series of project accounting reports for each contract, showing budget, estimate, contractual obligation, change orders, anticipated change orders, and estimated cost to complete; provide cost and payment status reports and report on the status of project reserve; monitor and report on expenditures against on-site overhead and general conditions budgets; furnish the owner detailed documentation of the total project cost at the completion of the project.

C   AGREEMENTS

1   Design Phase: Review the architect's and/or other consultants' contracts with the owner for coordination with this contract and establish a memorandum of understanding with the architect and/or other consultants to document mutual responsibilities.

Recommend division of work into separate contracts to permit phasing of the work, to assure that all work included in the plans and specifications is assigned to a contractor, and to prevent overlapping of responsibility; consider such factors as time and sequence of work, long lead-time materials and equipment, labor availability, trade jurisdictions, and local contracting practices. Establish a purchasing strategy for bidding or negotiating construction contracts.

Advise the owner on the need for soil and site surveys, inspections, and tests, and procure and manage these functions, if required. (CM does not assume responsibility for the accuracy and completeness of such reports and documents.)

Advise the owner on necessary permits, licenses, and bonds, and assist in obtaining them.

Assure that the contract documents contain provisions for temporary facilities, equipment, materials, and services for the common use of contractors.

2   Construction Phase: Observe work in progress and notify the architect or his engineers of any work that appears not to meet plans and specifications; consult the architect on interpretation if plans and specifications are unclear; direct contractors to check shop drawings for field conditions.

Negotiate change orders on behalf of the owner, maintain a file of all field orders, change order proposals, directives, and change orders.

Maintain a set of prints and specifications to reflect as-built conditions for use by the architect in producing record drawings; maintain an on-site library of sources for material, labor, services, approved shop drawings, and samples.

Assist the architect in the preparation of punch lists and review substantial completion documents before final processing.

Furnish the owner with all records, certificates, guarantees, warranties, and releases which are in CM's possession at the completion of the project.

CONTRACTS AND PROPOSALS

ARTICLE II—TERMS AND CONDITIONS OF PAYMENT

Two modes of payment are proposed as alternatives in this section of the CM contract. One is for payment of a fixed fee; the other bases the fee on a per cent of construction cost. Wording of the fixed fee contract is reproduced below. The percentage fee contract differs only by a paragraph inserted in Section A stipulating that, for purposes of calculating the fee, construction cost does not include CM, architectural or other professional fees or land costs, but it does include on-site costs of management and general conditions of construction. Any on-site labor, materials or fixed equipment furnished by the owner is also included at current market rates.

```
The owner will pay CM a fixed fee of $_____ plus reimbursement
of certain expenses as defined below.

A       FIXED FEE

The fee will be unaffected by variations between the estimate and the
bids or by change orders during the construction phase unless the owner
initiates an increase in scope.  In that event, the fee will be nego-
tiated based on the additional construction cost caused by the increase
in scope.

There are 2 phases to the work described in this contract:  precon-
struction and construction.  The preconstruction phase ends at the
award of the construction contract.  The compensation will equal 25% of
the total fixed fee plus reimbursable expenses for the preconstruction
phase.  There will be an initial payment of 5% when CM begins work on
the project.  Twenty percent (20%) will be divided into equal monthly
payments based on the most current schedule for the preconstruction
phase.  Seventy-five percent (75%) will be divided into equal monthly
payments based on the current schedule for the construction phase.
CM will prepare and periodically update for the owner's approval a
schedule of billings.

B       REIMBURSABLE EXPENSES

Compensation for reimbursable expenses is in addition to the fixed fee.
These expenses are incurred in the performance of the basic services.
A detailed estimate and accounting of all reimbursable expenses will be
prepared by CM for the owner's review and approval on the request of
the owner, but no later than the start of construction, and shall be
updated periodically as the project progresses.  Reimbursable expenses
include:

1       On-Site Management:  Consists of cost of management, technical,
and clerical personnel assigned to the on-site office, which may in-
clude but is not limited to the following: project manager, superin-
tendent, field manager, scheduler, estimator, accountant, secretary,
and clerk.  Such personnel may be assigned and become reimbursable
prior to the actual start of construction.

Cost of on-site personnel will be reimbursed at direct personnel
expense plus 50%.  (Direct personnel expense includes cost of salaries
and of mandatory and customary benefits, insurance, pensions, and
```

similar benefits, such as statutory employee benefits, and will be computed at 1.3 times the salary of the employee.) The personnel required for on-site management will be determined by CM subject to approval by the owner.

2   On-Site Office: Includes the cost of trailer, trailer utilities and sanitation, vehicles/mileage, telephone, postage, furniture and equipment, and supplies, plus the cost of appropriate insurance for these items.

3   Miscellaneous: Includes the cost of electronic data processing, expense of transportation and living when traveling in connection with the project, progress photographs, any employment agency fees for clerical, technical, and professional personnel hired for on-site office, and cost for relocation of personnel transferred to on-site office.

C   GENERAL CONDITIONS

If recommended by CM and approved by the owner, CM will provide or arrange for, in behalf of the owner, general conditions construction activities for the project. The owner will have the right to review and approve the general conditions budget prior to CM's initiating any commitment on the part of the owner. The owner will provide funds of a mutually agreed upon amount for a bank account for CM to use for direct payment of these expenses at cost. This account will be reimbursed monthly by the owner upon receipt of an itemized statement from CM. General conditions expenses may include but are not limited to: hauling, security, surveying, layout, temporary installations, storage, sanitation, roads, fences, barricades, safety, signs, parking, electricity, gas, water, elevators, hoists, cranes, small tools, fire protection, erosion control, weather protection, heat, cleaning, and installation of the owner's furnished items.

Cost will include the materials and equipment used in providing the general conditions items and the direct personnel expense of labor.

CM may furnish its own equipment at the site for performance of general conditions items, if available and approved by the owner. For these purposes, the rental rate on self-owned equipment will be as listed in the latest edition of the Associated Equipment Distributor's publication of nationally averaged rates.

D   PAYMENTS

Payments will be made monthly within 10 days after receipt of bill from CM. A service charge of 1½% per month will be added to the unpaid billing, beginning 30 days after the billing date. On accounts outstanding over 90 days, CM reserves the right to halt all construction management services and collect all documents (manuals, schedules, estimates, etc.) pertaining to the project until payment of the account is made in full. CM will not be held responsible for any costs or damages caused by CM's absence.

Records of CM's project expenses will be kept on a generally recognized accounting basis, and if requested, will be available to the owner or his authorized representative at mutually convenient times at CM's office.

No deductions will be made from CM's compensation on account of penalty, liquidated damages, or other sums withheld from payments to contractors.

E DELAY

If work is stopped more than 60 days by strike or other circumstances through no fault of CM, compensation for basic services during the stoppage beyond the 60th day will be computed as set forth in Article IV. In addition, the owner will compensate the staff, as provided for by this agreement, for the first 60 days of such stoppage. CM will reduce the size of its job-site staff for the remainder of the delay period as directed by the owner and, during that period, the owner will reimburse CM as determined in Article II, paragraph B, for the remaining on-site staff. Upon resumption of work, CM will restore the job-site staff to its appropriate size but will not guarantee that the staff will consist of the same individuals.

F SUSPENSION

If the project is suspended for 3 months or abandoned, CM will be paid its compensation then due, plus terminal expenses. If the project is resumed, CM's compensation will be subject to renegotiation.

G TERMINATION

Prior to completion of construction, this agreement may be terminated by either party upon 7 days' written notice should the other party fail substantially to perform in accordance with its terms through no fault of the other. In the event of termination by the owner, CM will be paid its compensation plus reimbursable expenses for services performed to termination date and all terminal expenses.

Terminal expenses are those directly attributable to termination (such as relocation costs) plus 10% of that portion of CM's fixed fee for the phase of work (preconstruction or construction) in progress not billed at the time of termination.

H COMPLETION

Completion of basic services described in this contract will be determined by issuance by the architect of the certificate of substantial completion, by occupancy of the building, or by final payment of all contractors.

If the owner requests, CM will continue all or a portion of its on-site management services for a reasonable length of time at the rate stipulated under Article II, paragraph B 1. Should the owner require basic services from CM beyond these on-site management services during the warranty period, CM will provide such services at 2.0 times the direct personnel expense plus direct expenses unless provided for under Article IV.

ARTICLE III
THE OWNER'S RESPONSIBILITIES

A REPRESENTATIVE

The owner will designate a representative to examine documents submitted by CM and render decisions and information promptly. CM may assume that all information and decisions furnished by the owner's representative are binding on the owner.

CONTRACTS AND PROPOSALS

B PROFESSIONAL SERVICES

The owner will furnish such legal, accounting, and insurance counseling services as required for the project.

The owner will retain an architect to design and prepare construction documents for the project. The architect will provide construction administration as is generally represented in one of the latest editions of AIA standard contracts between owner and architect. The extent of his duties and responsibilities and the limitations of his authority as assigned thereunder will not be modified without written agreement between the owner and CM.

C INSURANCE

The owner will obtain and maintain appropriate insurance in acceptable amounts throughout the project. He will file certificates of insurance with CM which include the following:

1 *Owner's Liability Insurance*: The owner will be responsible for purchasing and maintaining his own liability insurance and, at his option, may purchase and maintain such insurance as will protect him against claims which may arise from operations under the contract.

2 *Builders Risk and Property Insurance*: The owner will purchase and maintain builders risk and other property insurance upon the entire work at the site to its full insurable value. This insurance will include the interests of the owner, CM, contractors, subcontractors, and sub-subcontractors in the work and will be on a Broad Form All Risk of Physical Loss or Damage builders risk policy form.

The owner will purchase and maintain machinery, equipment, or other special coverage insurance as may be required by the contract documents or by law. This insurance will include the interest of the owner, CM, the contractors, subcontractors, and sub-subcontractors in the work.

D DOCUMENTS

The owner will give prompt written notice to CM whenever he becomes aware of any fault in the project or nonconformance with the contract documents.

ARTICLE IV
ADDITIONAL SERVICES

The following items, often associated with construction projects, are not part of the basic services. If any of the following additional services (or any other additional services) are authorized by the owner, they will be paid for by the owner at 3.0 times direct personnel expense of people involved in addition to their direct expenses.

A REPETITION

Repeating basic services for the project when such repetition is inconsistent with specific approvals or instructions previously given by the owner.

CONTRACTS AND PROPOSALS

B   OWNER'S CONSTRUCTION

Making detailed appraisals of existing facilities, making surveys or inventories required in connection with construction performed by the owner not managed under this contract. Providing services to investigate or making measured drawings of existing conditions or facilities, or verifying the accuracy of drawings or other information furnished by the owner.

C   DAMAGE TO THE WORK

Providing services required in connection with the replacement of work damaged by fire or other causes during construction.

D   EXPERT WITNESS

Preparing to serve and/or serving as an expert witness or preparing reports, evidence, giving depositions, or other assistance in connection with any public hearing, arbitration proceeding, or legal proceeding.

ARTICLE V
STIPULATIONS

A   FIXED LIMIT OF CONSTRUCTION COST

CM does not guarantee the accuracy of its cost estimates or that bids will not vary from any cost estimate. CM will not be liable or responsible to the owner or any other person for incidental or consequential damages of any nature resulting from its cost estimates.

If the owner establishes a written fixed limit of construction cost with the architect and CM, and if CM's estimate is below that fixed limit and bids exceed that fixed limit, then CM will, without additional charge, work with the owner and architect to modify the scope of the project and bring the construction cost within the fixed limit.

The fixed limit of construction cost may be established by letter agreement.

B   PROCUREMENT

CM will not bid on any construction work unless authorized by the owner. The work will be done by contractors under separate contract with the owner.

C   LOCATION

This agreement will be governed by the laws in effect in the state of Texas.

D   ASSOCIATION

Neither the owner nor CM will assign or transfer interest in the agreement without the written consent of the other; however, the construction manager may associate with another party in the performance of his services.

CONTRACTS AND PROPOSALS

E   EXTENT

This agreement is complete and supersedes prior representations or agreements.

Nothing herein will create a contractual relationship between CM and the architect or any contractors, subcontractors, or material suppliers on the project.

F   ARBITRATION

If both parties agree, disputes arising from this agreement will be decided by arbitration in accordance with the Construction Industry Arbitration Rules of the American Arbitration Association. This agreement to arbitrate will be specifically enforceable under the prevailing arbitration law. Notice of the demand for arbitration will be filed in writing with the other party to this agreement and with the American Arbitration Association. The demand will be made within a reasonable time after the dispute has arisen. In no event will the demand for arbitration be made after the date when institution of legal or equitable proceedings based on such claim, dispute, or other matter in question would be barred by the applicable statute of limitations. The award rendered by the arbitrators will be final, and judgment may be entered upon it in accordance with applicable law in any court having jurisdiction thereof.

G   CROSS-HIRING OF EMPLOYEES

The owner agrees not to hire or make any offer to hire any employee of CM during the term of the contract or within a year after termination of this contract.

This agreement entered into on _____, 19____.

CONSTRUCTION MANAGER   OWNER

_____   _____

_____   _____

By_____   _____

Title_____   Title_____

Date_____   Date_____

It is apparent from the foregoing that contracts and proposals for construction management are reaching a maturity that provides the basis for permanent resolution of some of the conflicts that have beset development of the construction management concept.

CONTRACTUAL RELATIONSHIPS: VARIATIONS ON A THEME

The construction management contract must be adaptable to a variety of organizational relationships that affect the lines of professional agency toward the owner. These lines of agency (four common arrangements are illustrated below) in turn affect the performance of some of the basic services listed in the prototype contracts previously outlined.

Bradford Perkins, writing as a member of the firm of McKee-Berger-Mansueto in the October, 1973, issue of *Architectural Record* (Perkins later became managing partner of Llewelyn-Davies Associates), points out that some construction managers have thought they were called upon to do a

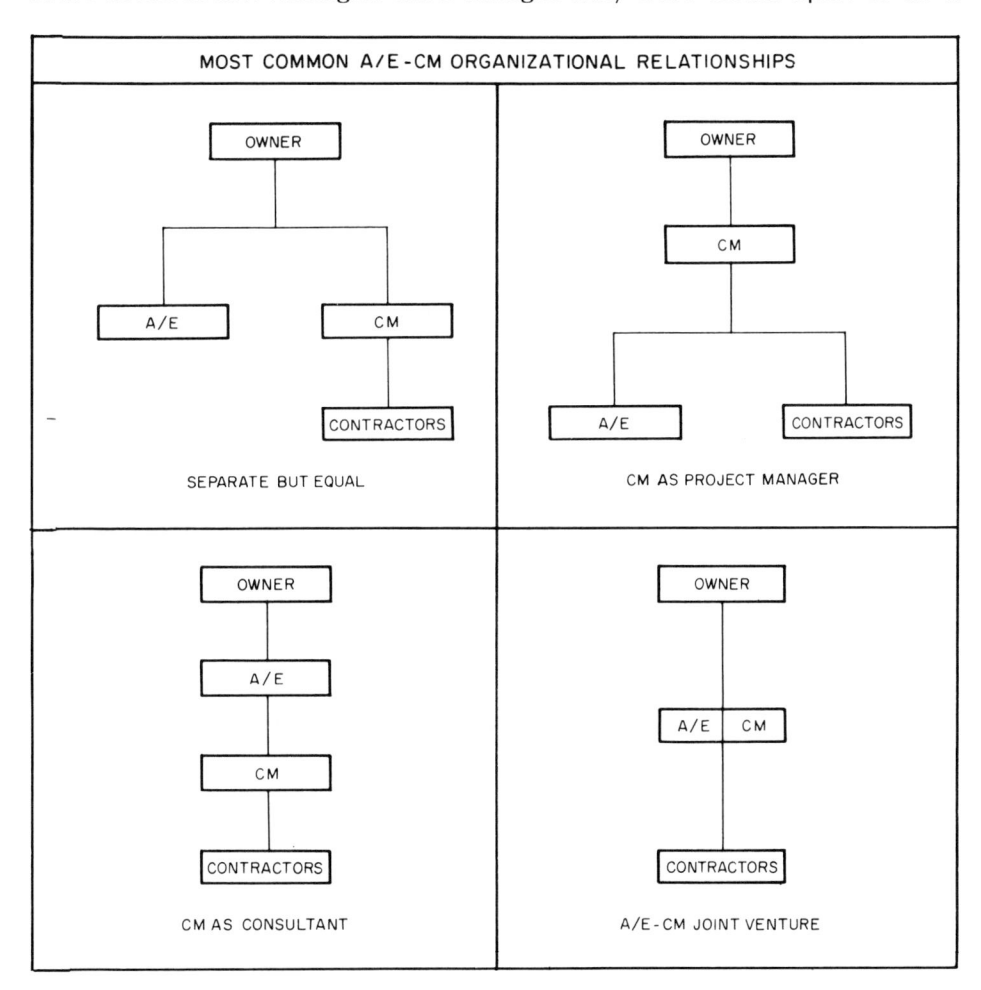

MOST COMMON A/E-CM ORGANIZATIONAL RELATIONSHIPS

SEPARATE BUT EQUAL

CM AS PROJECT MANAGER

CM AS CONSULTANT

A/E-CM JOINT VENTURE

number of time-consuming tasks normally performed by the A/E (though not necessarily spelled out in his agreement). These tasks have to do with document flow and checking as well as many on-site services that must be performed by the firm most involved at the site—now usually the CM.

"One point that should be remembered," says Perkins, "is that the notion of basic services is a surrender of clarity to convenience. There is no such thing as a typical job, and the service definitions in standard contracts—good as those contracts may otherwise be—are a lazy man's approach. Every job has different requirements, and every combination of owner, A/E and CM has different capabilities. Therefore, for a successful contractual relationship, the project professionals should work out a clear definition of each group's function and responsibility in as much detail as possible before the contracts are executed. Standard agreements make good boiler plate, but a clear service definition makes up the boiler's working parts."

This clarity of contract goes further than simply expediting the project. It is a check against any overlap of liability. McKee-Berger-Mansueto sometimes inserts the following clauses to further clarify that liability position:

A. The services which shall be performed by MBM pursuant to the provisions of this Agreement shall not constitute MBM an architect, engineer or contractor nor impose upon MBM any obligation to assume . . . (duties or obligations) . . . except for the provisions of this Agreement nor impose upon MBM any liability with respect thereto.

B. Nothing contained herein shall be construed to impose upon MBM any liability with respect to the performance of the services referred to in the section on Inspection . . . (nor for the work, performance or certifications that are clearly the responsibility of contractors, architects or engineers on the project).

These clauses simply underscore the classic roles of participants, none of which are pre-empted by the CM. Nor do they imply that the CM has no liability exposure. "He does, of course, but these are limited to his own services as spelled out in his own contract."

7 | COMPUTERS IN PERSPECTIVE

Computers play a dual role as tools for time, cost and quality control in construction management. First, they serve as high-speed mathematical aids—especially in the areas of engineering, estimating and scheduling. Second, computers are a sorting, collating and reporting tool for the management process. They can relate the emplacement schedule to, for example, purchasing, cash flow, inspections, meetings and approvals. The special conditions of client procedures, the myriad variations in emphasis and detail for communicating the same body of information to, say, the contractor, the purchasing agent and the project administrator; all can be sorted out by the computer with idiot speed and with no more error than its human masters feed into its programs.

The computer can make infinite lists. It can list all the systems and activities in a project in several ways: by date of early or late start in a CPM network, by longest-lead time for purchasing, by cost, by supplier, by contractor or (for the project administrator) by over-all summary of cost and schedule.

This listing and sorting process is perhaps the least demanding on the potential skills of the computer and its programmers. It has been called a trivial use of great capacity. But it can be, on complex projects, the computer's most rewarding use in terms of savings in time and money; in terms of coordinated communications; and in terms of evaluating the cost/quality options.

The myth of the computer as super-machine that takes over all tasks and has its accomplishments measured in stacked feet of print-out paper is long past. Now the machine is more maturely regarded as a high-level investment in the *profitable* (i.e. rapid) manipulation of *massive* and *relevant* data. It has a mindless talent for repetitive scanning, with key (and keyed) variations in either the core-memory of applied parameters or the daily input of job data.

But building design and construction are exceptionally non-repetitive—in comparison with manufacturing or accounting procedures. Although both manufacturing and accounting are within the purview of construction management, the idiosyncracies of each job and each client call for rigorous assessment of the computer's applicability job by job. The key words underscored in the preceding paragraph are: *profitable*, *massive*, and *relevant*.

There are two major considerations that bear on the construction manager's assessment of computer applicability.

1. No management program can be turned over to a computer to the total exclusion of manual calculation and verbal communication. Someone has to read the print-out, make decisions, write reports and orders, negotiate, see that things get done. Even cost estimating, a chore of massive detail that would seem readily amenable to computerization, becomes progressively more refined and immediate, (and therefore more costly to program) as documents develop—to the point where estimating and negotiation (and sometimes redesign) are virtually concomitant—the point, in fact, where the real price is the bid price. Computerized costing is a well developed service, but there comes a time on every project when the computer must give way to the pencil sharpener.

2. The smaller the project, the larger is the proportion of manual and verbal (i.e., non-computerized) component in the management task. Considering the difference between, say, the World Trade Center and a $500,000 factory, that seems a simplistic statement. But somewhere on the scale of size and complexity between those two extremes is a point below which no job-developed software is warranted—no matter how much in-house hardware is standing by to handle it. The location of that point is itself a management decision based on the answer to a simple question. Does it pay?

The answer to that question is not always revealed by simple arithmetic.

It can be distorted by two opposing attitudes. One that has cost untold amounts in overkill is the compulsion to "keep the hardware busy." The other, equally costly, has been a reluctance to use expensive and exotic machines in the trivial role of giant tickler file. A judgment must be made based on the particulars of:

1) available hardware in-house,
2) its cost to own or rent,
3) its current loading,
4) software programming cost for the project,
5) available core programs,
6) management demands of the project,
7) management fees available,

plus the particulars of manpower and current work load of the management firm itself.

At risk of offering figures that are dated and otherwise limited by special conditions, we report the following yardsticks of computer cost mentioned at a 1971 seminar of the Advanced Management Research International.

1. Engineering firms with repetitive usage of well developed programs and good load factor spend about $40 per month per graduate engineer on staff.

2. The cost of in-house hardware is about one-third to one-half of the cost of computing; the rest goes into people, programming, supplies and space.

3. A minimum cost for in-house hardware alone is between $1500 and $2000 per month.

4. Initial cost for time-sharing at a service center is much less, but the added cost of communication and travel brings the total to almost $1500—not counting personnel.

The two major considerations previously stated having to do with the limits of computer application (i.e.: no program can be 100 per cent computerized; and small projects may not warrant any computerization at all) set the stage for developing management systems for cost, quality and time control using the computer at key points. Those points are determined by the criteria of project characteristics in size and complexity and by the resources of the managing firm itself.

The ideal management system would be totally flexible so that it could be applied logically and economically over a full scale of job and firm criteria. It turns out, however, that the development of a computer-oriented system capable of serving the management of large projects calls for a certain commitment of the management firm to full-time staffing for computer programming, cost estimating and field operating personnel. That commitment sets a high break-even point that almost automatically precludes the handling of small projects except on a fragmentary basis. Such a firm might, for example, accept a commission for periodic cost estimating, or for CPM consultation. But these fragmentary services, however genuine and useful, are not to be confused with what has been defined as full-scale professional construction management.

For those who are concerned about the role of the small professional firm on small projects, it should be pointed out that the basic functions of all of the services of construction management listed so far have been performed routinely by architects, engineers, contractors and others within conventional fee structures. It is only size, complexity, and urgency that create a milieu in which the role of the professional construction manager emerges as a separate and separately charged profession. So, if we now address ourselves to the components of management systems for larger works, those who are so inclined may scale their own activities to those components that seem feasibly separable.

The role of the computer as mathematical calculator in engineering and accounting fields has been amply documented elsewhere. It is upon the role of reporter and collator in project administration and construction management that fresh judgments must be brought to bear. Because of the virtually infinite capacity of the machine to respond, the dangers of both overkill and underemployment must be dealt with.

COMPONENTS OF THE COMPUTERIZED MANAGEMENT SYSTEM

A well-designed management system for the control of construction projects will combine capabilities in cost estimating, critical path analysis, financial status and progress reports, and administrative procedures in a well-organized format. Individual reports should be designed for each level of project administration and construction management. In each case, the system should be able to use either a manual or a computerized mode of reporting in order to approach as closely as practicable the kind of ideal flexibility previously described. (See also PBS-CMCS system, page 85-86.)

Because of the mass of data available and the immense capability of the machine to absorb and report, an essentially editorial judgment should be made as to content and format of these reports. That judgment should be based on the function and preoccupation of individual recipients. For example, the project administrator might receive a summary schedule and financial status report while the on-site construction manager would require a more detailed list of all work items for each phase of the job.

Individual reports and input documents should not only be tailored to each user but should also have consistent format one with another, so that

COMPUTERS IN PERSPECTIVE

```
** TICKLER FILE SAMPLE **

NAME   AREA   DATE       DESCRIPTION
RC     UTLB   01/01/71   PRE - ORDER EQUIP - UTILITY BUILDING EQUIPMENT
RC     UTIL   01/01/72   ADVERTISE - COOLING WATER PIPING
RC     SITE   01/01/72   ADVERTISE - FINE GRADING & LANDSCAPE
TOT    080    01/05/71   NOTICE TO PROCEED                               -SCIENCE
TOT    080    01/20/71   START WORK                                      -SCIENCE
RC     MDC    02/01/71   COMPLETE FINAL DESIGN      - MDC
RC     UTLB   02/01/72   START WORK - UTILITY BUILDING EQUIPMENT
RC     UTIL   02/01/72   START WORK - COOLING WATER PIPING
RC     SITE   02/01/72   START WORK - FINE GRADING & LANDSCAPE
RC     MDC    03/01/71   ADVERTISE                  - MDC
RC     SDS    03/01/71   PRE FINAL DESIGN - SDS
RC     SITE   03/01/71   SET UP PLANT - CONCRETE BATCH PLANT
RC     SITE   03/01/71   SET UP LAB - TESTING LAB
RC     SDS    04/01/71   FINAL DESIGN - SDS
RC     SDS    04/01/72   INSTALL - SDS
RC     MDC    04/15/71   START WORK                 - MDC
RC     SDS    05/01/71   ADVERTISE - SDS
TOT    080    08/21/70   FUME HOOD SPECS, DRAFT                          -SCIENCE
TOT    080    08/21/70   LAB FURNITURE,PRE QUALIF DWGS & SPECS           -SCIENCE
TOT    080    08/21/70   BBC ACCEPTANCE OF PRE QUALIF PROCEDURES         -SCIENCE
JM     020    08/21/70   FOOD SERVICE INFO FROM C7A              -COLLEGE 020
DT     090    08/24/70   REV PRE FINAL ESTIMATE - LIBRARY
TOT    080    08/24/70   BUDGET FIGURES FOR LAB EQUIP & FUME HOODS       -SCIENCE
JM     020    08/24/70   MECH & ELEC DRAWINGS FROM COSENTINI     -COLLEGE 020
```

Giant tickler and ultimate sorting machine—a trivial use, perhaps, of all that sophisticated electronic gear—the computer performs its most frequent role in that service for construction management. The printouts fractionally reproduced here and on following pages demonstrate the machine's ability to make lists in almost any array of category its masters may require. The text explains the goals of these permutations. Most of the exhibits are by courtesy of MBM. Exceptions are the bar-chart variations of CPM network information on pages 100 and 101 and the contract bid schedule on page 106, which are by courtesy of Amis Construction and Consultation Services, Inc.

translation of data into decision and action is handled readily.

The information presented by the system should be coordinated on the basis of a scheduled flow of input related to stipulated intervals and classifications of output. That is, the data sources, such as estimators, field inspectors, job captains, clerks of the works, etc., should be encouraged to report back to the system at stipulated intervals and in patterned format readily convertible to input data.

A workable system might be designed to present four basic areas of information (schedule, cost, financial and administrative) to three key decision-making groups: project administration, construction management and a third-level comparable to job captain or field superintendent which might be labeled "technical management." Definition of the four areas of information might be amplified as follows:

A. Scheduling, planning, and control of project duration usually employs the CPM technique or one of its variations. The system should develop a detailed model of each project's design-delivery-occupancy process as a single identity made up of many parts. The network technique both views the process as a whole and separates its parts into manageable modules.

B. Cost control systems should present timely cost data in useful format. These data are exceptionally sensitive to the chance conditions of the market and the phase of design development. For that reason, its reporting method usually has a high manual component.

C. Financial summaries integrate data generated in the estimating and scheduling areas in order to show how much of the project's total cost has been spent and how much will be committed in designated future periods. These summaries also indicate the extent to which funding and cash flow has been approved and appropriated.

D. The administrative applications of the system tend to be less rigidly structured than other areas and are tailored to the in-house capabilities and methods of the owner and/or project administrator. In order to provide full services to a variety of clients, public and private, over a substantial spread of project size, the construction management firm should be prepared to fit its own capabilities to those of the client. The danger lies in overstaffing for a level of administrative participation that may not be required to a consistent degree from one client to another.

Some of the administrative backup services to be considered might include manuals of procedure, either general to the construction management process or specific for the project at hand, outlines of useful administrative reports, step-by-step procedures and background literature on construction markets and practices that may be helpful to the less sophisticated client. Again, the service should be tailored to the need.

DATE -31MAY71
DATA DATE-31MAY71

MULTI-PROJECT FINANCIAL STATUS REPORT

PAGE- 3

(ALL VALUES TO NEAREST $1000)

PROJECT	BUDGET A	ESTIM COST AT COMPLETE B	OVER(-) UNDER C=A-B	CONTRACT AMOUNT D	RESERVAT OF FUNDS E	APPROVED PAYMENTS F	UNPAID COMMITS G=D-F	RESERVAT OF FUNDS BALANCE H=E-F	COMMITS TO COMPLETE I=A-D
BUS BUS TERMINAL - D /ESIGN & CONSTRUCT		1,248	1,248-	96	11	16	80	5-	96-
CONT ESCALATION FOR D /ELAY(METHANE STUDY		2,500	2,500-						-
LAND LAND COST /.		1,900	1,900-						-
METH METHANE GAS STUD /IES & SYST DESIGN		310	310-	30	596	511	481-	85	30-
MGT MANAGEMENT FEES /.		2,295	2,295-		1,813	1,492	1,492-	321	-
PO PROJECT OFFICE C /OSTS(INCL SITE)		1,875	1,875-	4	991	525	522-	465	4-
PROJ TOTAL PROJECT BU /DGBT	130,000		130,000						130,000
SITE SITE WORK AND UT /ILITIES		17,335	17,335-	11,694	7,453	3,292	8,402	4,161	11,694-
SOIL SITE AND SOILS I /NVESTIGATIONS		874	874-	285	751	646	360-	105	285-
010 COLLEGB BUILDING /.		22,172	22,172-	3,510	953	848	2,662	105	3,510-
020 COULEGB BUILDING		21,494	21,494-	19,042	17,666	824	18,219	16,842	19,042-

COMPUTERS IN PERSPECTIVE

USEFUL MANAGEMENT REPORTS

In order to discipline the unlimited computer output at a manageable level, the professional construction manager should establish specific sets of reports. These reports will draw upon the complete reservoir of project data, but will be assembled in format relating the four categories of information previously described to the needs of recipients. The reports will also be tailored to the management level to which they are directed.

Top-level reports. Most major projects have a senior decision-making group made up of client representatives, and principals of the architectural, engineering and construction management firms. Ordinarily, these people have more than one center of interest in addition to the project itself. Their objective as a group is to maintain adequate surveillance of the project development in order to respond intelligently when top level decisions are required. Useful reports for this group should give clear and concise information about a project's general progress, its cost status related to the schedule and its financial status related to the budget. This information might be usefully divided into:

1) A narrative report from the principal in charge of construction management, summarizing overall development and pointing up significant problems that might call for action of the top management group;

2) A financial-status report summarizing critical aspects of the budget-schedule relationship, noting any significant change between the current and prior period, alerting management to any need for additional or progress funding;

3) A master schedule chart in some readily comprehensible form (usually a bar chart) which serves as a summary of current status of the CPM schedule condensing all significant aspects of the project delivery process through a display of key activities.

Action-level reports. At the second level of management, directly related full-time to the project, is a second category of reports also tailored to the problems of the individuals concerned. The objective is to avoid inundating all members of this management echelon with the massive data typical of large projects. The "need to know" principle should be applied to the editing of these reports, which might include:

1) A narrative report based on cost and progress information from the field or from "technical management" summarizing current developments;

2) A summary of the master schedule detailing activities of the network for the entire project and serving as a central scheduling checklist for the project;

3) A critical list of items within the network with minimal float time that must be watched most carefully; *(text continued on page 118)*

COMPUTERS IN PERSPECTIVE

```
RUN DATE 30 JUL 71      **           B A R   G R A P H           **        DATA DATE  01 AUG 71
RUN SEQUENCE 1  NETWORK ID  1         COLONY SQUARE MASTER NETWORK         FROM  01 AUG 71  TO  01 MAR 72
SEQUENCE  E S                                                                    PAGE    1        PART  1

     *  DURATION,  X  CRITICAL DURATION,  -  FLOAT,  N  NEGATIVE FLOAT

                                                              MTWTFSS  MTWTFSS  MTWTFSS  MTWTFSS  MTWTFSS  MTWTFSS
  W I    D E S C R I P T I O N            WORK ITEM           26JUL71  09AUG71  23AUG71           06SEP71
-----------------------------------------------------------------------------------------------------------------
STAFFING & MANPOWER REASSIGNMENTS         2A2   ARCH          I        XXXXX    I        I        I        I
STAFFING & MANPOWER REASSIGNMENTS         2B2   MECH          I        *****    -----    -        -        -
STAFFING & MANPOWER REASSIGNMENTS         2C2   STRT          I        *****    -----    -        I        I
AUTHORIZE ADDITIONAL BORINGS              2E2   OWNR          *        -----    -        -        -        -
CENTRAL POWER PLANT - ASSUME YES          2F2   OWNR          *        -----    -        -        -        -
ROOF TOP RESTAURANT - ASSUME NO           2G2   OWNR          *        -----    -        I        I        I
NOTICE TO PROCEED                         2H1                 I        -        -        -        -        -
THIRD FLOOR TENANT - ASSUME NO            2H2   OWNR          *        -----    -        -        -        -
START APTS AND CONIMINIUM                 3G1                 I        I        I        I        I        I
START WORK ON MALL AND PLAZA              5G1                 I        -        -        -        -        -
RINK OR POOL DECISION                     5J2   OWNR          *        *****    -----    -        -        -
SELECT GARAGE SECURITY SYSTEM             6C2   OWNR          I        *****    *****    *****    *****    I
ADJACENT PARKING ACCESS - ASSUME NO       6D2   OWNR          I        *****    -----    -        -        -
DEFINE HOTEL PARKING REQUIREMENTS         6E2   OWNR          I        *****    -----    -        -        -
START GARAGE                              6G1                 I        I        I        I        I        I
PRESENTATION TO SITY - PEACHTREE ACCESS   6G2   ARCH          *        *****    -----    -        -        -
RESOLVE MODE OF OPERATING GARAGE          6H2   OWNR          I        *-----   -        -        -        -
RESOLVE RETAIL AREA AND LAYOUT            6J2   OWNR          I        *****    -----    -        -        -
CONSTRUCTION TRAFFIC PROBLES AT 100 COL. SG.  6J7  ARCH       I        *****    *****    *****    *****    I
RESOLVE RESTAURANT LOCATION AND SIZE      6K2   OWNR          I        *****    -----    -        -        -
RESOLVE GARAGE TRAFFIC CONTROL            6L2   OWNR          I        **---    -        -        -        -
RESOLVE MATERIAL HANDLING IN GARAGE       6M2   OWNR          I        *-----   -        -        -        -
RESOLVE TRUCK DOCKING                     6N2   OWNR          I        *-----   -        -        -        -
MATERIAL VERIFICATION                     6N3   CONT          I        *****    -----    -        -        -
ESTIMATE - RETAINING WALL                 6P3   CONT          I        *****    -----    -        -        -
SCHEMATIC ESTIMATE HOTEL                  8C1   CONT          I        *****    *****    *****    *****    I
PRELIM REVIEW-ZONING & BLDG INSP-HOTEL    8D2   ARCH          I        *****    *****    *****    *****    I
START HOTEL                               8G1                 I        -        -        -        -        -
UTILITY DECISIONS FOR HOTEL               8K2   OWNR          I        *****    -----    -        -        -
START 400 COLONY SQUARE                   4H1                 I        I----    -        -        -        -
ADD'L BORINGS                             4E2   ARCH          I        *****    -        -        -        -
HIRE SPEC WRITER                          4J2   ARCH          I        *****    *****    *****    *****    I
```

112 COMPUTERS IN PERSPECTIVE

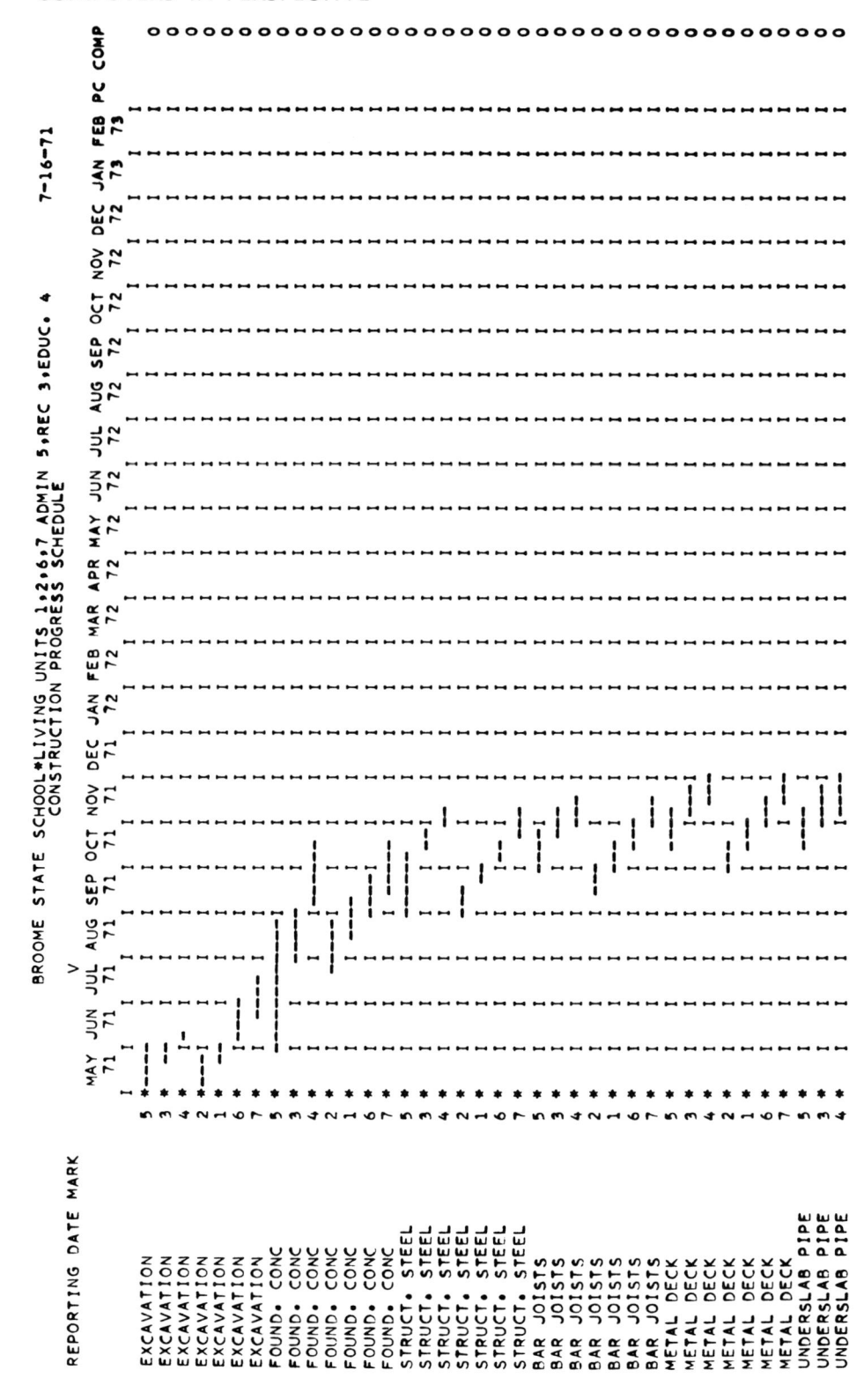

BROOME STATE SCHOOL*LIVING UNITS 1,2,6,7 ADMIN 5,REC 3,EDUC. 4 7-16-71
CONSTRUCTION PROGRESS SCHEDULE

COMPUTERS IN PERSPECTIVE

CAPITOL DISTRICT CENTER — BOILER PLANT
CONSTRUCTION PROGRESS SCHEDULE

8- 3-71

[Gantt-style construction progress schedule chart spanning MAR 71 through DEC 72, with activities listed vertically including: EXCAVATION, SHEETING, POROUS PIPE & FILL, UNDERSLAB PIPE, UNDERSLAB CONDUIT, MAT, EQUIPMENT PADS, RIGGING, CONC IM SUPERSTRUCT., P/C STRUCTURE TEES, INTERIOR MASONRY, ROOFING & S.M., HOLLOW METAL EXT, PLASTER, CEILING, PAINTING & FINISHING, FLOORING, PLUMBING, PLMBG. EQUIP., PLMBG. FIXT., H.V.&A.C, H.V.&A.C EQUIP., H.V.&A.C DUCT., H.V.&A.C DIFF., CONTROLS, FUEL OIL TANKS, PIPING, STACK, ELECTRIC, ELECT. EQUIP., LIGHT FIXTURES, SITE WORK, PUNCH LIST. Percent complete column shows values: 100, 100, 60, 100, 0, 100, 0, 0, 5, 0, 0, ... with remaining activities at 0.]

LEGEND:
——— 1ST BAR 1-7, 2ND BAR 8-15, 3RD BAR 16-22, 4TH BAR 23-30
——— SCHED. ACTIVITY, XXX ACTUAL ACTIVITY, 000 PROJECTED ACTIVITY

113

MULTI PROJECT CURRENT WORKING ESTIMATE

DATE - 31MAY71
DATA DATE- 31MAY71
PAGE- 1

PROJECT	ORIGINAL COST ESTIMATE A	APPROVED CHANGE ORDERS B	REVISED CUMMULATIVE COST ESTIMATE C=A+B	ESTIMATED COST AT COMPLETION D	OVER(-) UNDER E=C-D
BUS BUS TERMINAL - DESIGN & CONSTRUCT	1,110,000		1,110,000	1,110,000	
CONT ESCALATION FOR DELAY(METHANE STUDY	2,500,000		2,500,000	2,500,000	
LAND LAND COST	1,900,000		1,900,000	1,900,000	
SITE SITE WORK AND UTILITIES	15,334,459	12,546	15,347,005	15,347,005	
SOIL SITE AND SOILS INVESTIGATIONS	874,100	11,414-	862,686	862,686	
010 COLLEGE BUILDING	19,000,000		19,000,000	19,000,000	
020 COLLEGE BUILDING	18,446,750		18,446,750	18,446,750	

*** PROJECT FILE ***
(ALL VALUES SHOWN TO NEAREST $1000)

DATE- 31MAY71
PAGE- 1 PART 1

BLDG NO	TITLE	BUDGET ESTIMATE CURRENT PREVIOUS	CHANGE	DESIGN FEE	C/O CONT.	OVER HEAD	MGT	FURN	OTHER	TOTAL (EPC)
BUS	BUS TERMINAL - D /ESIGN & CONSTRUCT	1,110 1,110		96	33	10				1,248
CONT	ESCALATION FOR D /ELAY(METHANE STUDY	2,500 2,500								2,500
LAND	LAND COST	1,900 1,900								1,900

DATE- 31MAY71
*** PROJECT FILE ***
(ALL VALUES SHOWN TO NEAREST $1000)
PAGE- 1 PART 2

BLDG NO	TITLE	TOTAL (EPC)	CUMMULATIVE TO-DATE CONTR	R/F	INV	COS	APP COS	PREVIOUS PERIOD CONTR	R/F	INV	COS	APP COS
BUS	BUS TERMINAL - D /ESIGN & CONSTRUCT	1,248		11	16				11	16		
CONT	ESCALATION FOR C /ELAY(METHANE STUDY	2,500										
LAND	LAND COST	1,900										
SITE	SITE WORK AND UT /ILITIES	17,335	10,771	7,453	3,292	13	13	10,771	7,452	2,659	28-	28-
SOIL	SITE AND SOILS I /NVESTIGATIONS	874	285	751	646	11-	11-	285	751	646	11-	11-
010	COLLEGE BUILDING	22,172	2,361	953	848			2,361	953	819		
020	COLLEGE BUILDING	21,494	17,967	17,666	824			17,967	17,657	824		
080	SCIENCE BUILDING	25,640	19,889	20,748	945			19,889	20,748	945		
090	LIBRARY AND PLAZ /A	19,327	1,140	2,111	1,780	90	90	1,140	2,111	1,780	90	90
110	ADMINISTRATION B /UILDING	5,804	4,862	4,861	251			4,862	4,861	251		
150	CENTRAL SERVICES / BUILDING	4,753	3,122	3,023	197	62-	62-	3,122	3,014	197		
	UNALLOCATED EXPE /NSES	766		6,146	3,766	30	30		6,146	2,690		
TOTALS		127,793	60,431	67,123	15,093			60,431	66,914	13,063	51	51 (000)

DATE 31MAY71   PROGRAMMED CONTRACT COSTS   PAGE 1
                                                                                                    PART 1

CONTRACT NO	TITLE	CURRENT CONSTRUCTION ESTIMATE	ACTUAL AWARD COST	CHANGE ORDER CONTINGENCY	FEE ESTIMATE	OTHER COSTS ESTIMATE	CURENT TOTAL COST
2-1	ACCESS RD & FENCING		77,317	7,700	8,178	2,360	95,555
2-2	EXCAVATION		535,500	53,500	33,201	13,300	635,501
2-3	GRADING & DIKE CONSTRUCTION		5,484,342	274,000	319,737	69,000	6,147,079
2-4	UTILITY EQUIPMENT & DISTRIBUTION S		4,674,000	235,000	276,233	18,000	5,203,233
2-7	ROADWORK, WALKS, ETC.	1,423,500		99,650	76,727	11,524	1,611,401
2-8	FINAL GRADING AND LANDSCAPING	626,800		50,144	37,921	14,040	728,905
2-9	SUPERVISORY DATA SYSTEM	848,000		67,840	59,869	6,000	981,709
2-10	TEMPORARY RAMP	177,000		12,390	13,310	6,016	208,716
2-11	UTILITY BUILDING	1,488,000		119,040	98,059	18,072	1,723,171
2B1	RODENT CONTROL		6,930				6,930
2B2	TEST PILES & SOILS LAB		212,900	220		500	213,180
2B6	TEMR ELECT FACILITIES		3,660				3,660
2B7	METHANE STUDY. - LAMBE		15,000				15,000
2B8	METHANE STUDY - HEDBNBERG & VENABL		10,000				10,000
2B9	METHANE STUDY - GERMANTOWN LABS		5,000				5,000
2B10	SOILS, HUB TESTING LABS.		30,080				30,080
2B11	SOILS, J.P. COLLINS & ASSOC		18,447				18,447
2B12	SOILS, LAMBE ASSOC		17,000				17,000
3-1	PILES		1,624,745	81,300	127,380	7,000	1,840,425

DATE 31MAY71　　　　　ACTUAL CONTRACT COSTS　　　　　PAGE 1
　　　　　　　　　　　　　　　　　　　　　　　　　　　　PART 2

CONTRACT NO	CONSTRUCTION PERCENT COMPLETE	PAID	RETAINED	CHANGE ORDERS APPROVED	DESIGN PERCENT COMPLETE	FEES PAID	OTHER COSTS	TOTAL COST	BALANCE ON CONTRACT	VARIANCE FROM PROGRAM
2-1		111,730	5,042	23,518				116,772	21,217	5,280
2-2		514,433	23,890	51,236				538,323	97,178	151,237
2-3		2,152,774	101,762	40,263				2,254,537	3,892,542	622,474
2-4		134,645						134,645	5,068,588	529,233
2-7		31,463						31,463	1,579,938	187,901
2-8		4,521						4,521	724,384	102,105
2-9									981,709	133,709
2-10									208,716	31,716
2-11		63,738						63,738	1,659,433	235,171
2B1		4,620						4,620	2,310	
2B2		201,766	10,074	11,414				211,840	1,340	11,694
2B6		3,527		133				3,527	133	133
2B7		14,828						14,828	172	
2B8		8,969						8,969	1,031	
2B9		3,721						3,721	1,279	
2B10		30,080						30,080		
2B11		18,439						18,439	8	
2B12		16,802						16,802	198	
3-1		4,541						4,541	1,835,884	215,680

COMPUTERS IN PERSPECTIVE　　117

```
                        CONTRACT + BID SCHEDULE                        1 OF45
                        -----------------------
       BROOME STATE SCHOOL*LIVING UNITS 1,2,6,7 ADMIN 5,REC 3,EDUC. 4    7-16-71 R.0
***********************************************************************************
*                       * DESIGN * C O N T R A C T * S H O P   D W G S* REQ'D  * N *
*                       * READY  ********************************************* ON   * O *
*     T R A D E         * 100./.*ADV. PR.* AWARD  * PREP. +* APPR.  * JOB    * T *
*         +             *        * + BID  *        * SUBM. *          *        * E *
*      I T E M          *        *        *        *        *         *        *   *
***********************************************************************************
*                       *        *        *        *        *         *        *   *
*EXCAVATION         5   *        * 6 WKS  * 2 WKS  *        *         * 0 WKS  *   *
*                       * 3- 8-71* 4-19-71* 5- 3-71* NOT REQUIRED      * 5- 3-71* L *
*                       *        *        *        *        *         *        *   *
*FOUND. CONC       3   *        * 8 WKS  * 1 WKS  * 3 WKS  * 1 WKS   * 1 WKS  *   *
*                       * 4-26-71* 6-21-71* 6-28-71* 7-19-71* 7-26-71 * 8- 2-71*   *
*                       *        *        *        *        *         *        *   *
*FOUND. CONC       4   *        * 8 WKS  * 1 WKS  * 3 WKS  * 1 WKS   * 1 WKS  *   *
*                       * 5-31-71* 7-26-71* 8- 2-71* 8-23-71* 8-30-71 * 9- 6-71*   *
*                       *        *        *        *        *         *        *   *
*FOUND. CONC       2   *        * 8 WKS  * 1 WKS  * 3 WKS  * 1 WKS   * 1 WKS  *   *
*                       * 4-19-71* 6-14-71* 6-21-71* 7-12-71* 7-19-71 * 7-26-71*   *
*                       *        *        *        *        *         *        *   *
*FOUND. CONC       1   *        * 8 WKS  * 1 WKS  * 3 WKS  * 1 WKS   * 1 WKS  *   *
*                       * 5-10-71* 7- 5-71* 7-12-71* 8- 2-71* 8- 9-71 * 8-16-71*   *
*                       *        *        *        *        *         *        *   *
***********************************************************************************
```

Portion of Amis chart for job control. L at right (first item) is for late.

4) *(Text continued from page 110)* A list of important dates on individual system schedules of the project;

5) An alerting list of key activities scheduled to take place within the immediate future; a period of, say, 60 to 90 days, in a print-out arranged in sequence by early start date;

6) A master tickler for central management summarizing the upcoming activities of staff and compiled from the individual tickler files of staff members in a uniform format;

7) Current working estimates bringing out significant detail from the data used as background for the top management cost and financial status reports;

8) Detailed current cost estimates identifying building system costs and noting changes from the preceding period to readily spot any system in danger of a cost overrun;

9) A cash flow summary providing a monthly check against schedule activity and not only projecting cash flow requirements but implementing the payment process for upcoming schedules.

The sorting and format of these reports, the intervals of their issuance, and the lists of individuals to whom they are directed are all subject to the characteristics of the project and the organization of the management firm itself. Computer print-outs are not the most readable of documents, although as users become familiar with them and programmers edit their physical volume to manageable dimensions, they become increasingly useful. A few examples of the forementioned types of reports are illustrated.

ROLE OF THE COMPUTER IN COST CONTROL

The multiplicity of items and parameters in cost estimating and control would seem to be a logical background for enlistment of the computer. It turns out, however, that such variables as local market conditions, labor productivity, local shop rules and the flux of price and product change itself are so ephemeral that the cost of monitoring and programming for a completely automated estimating system is likely to be disproportionate—especially for private, one-shot work.

Nevertheless, there have been several public and private attempts to computerize various portions of the estimating process. Notable federal commissions in this area have been issued by NASA and the Navy. The regional experiment by New York state to monitor not only building costs but also current loading on the construction market has been described. Some private firms have developed computerized estimating systems based on cost histories and various modifying parameters that seem to work fairly well in various stages of the automating process. It is quite likely that as estimating becomes more and more critical to the design and delivery of buildings under the conditions of phased construction, the economics of monitoring the local market and programming the computer for a fuller role will shift toward greater profitability.

Estimating occurs at three levels: 1) The detailed working estimate where a take-off of all materials by quantity and price gives an accurate cost for the job; 2) The estimate at the systems level is an integration of experience that tells how much a heating system or a structural system should cost; 3) The estimate at the concept level is another scale of integrated experience that tells how much a warehouse or a hospital or other building type should cost. Any attempt at computerization should take into account the fact that, in addition to material and labor costs, there are dozens of modifying indicators pertaining to the time, place, and conditions of the work.

At one time, the real estate and construction division of IBM developed a list of about 850 specific items of construction components on which they computerized the cost history building by building over the more than 100 buildings of the corporation all over the world. After two years of capturing data on actual costs in place for hundreds of buildings, they applied sophisticated computerized techniques of analysis and found little or no correlation on an item by item basis from building to building. Further search revealed that the reason for this discrepancy was primarily a function of inconsistency in contractors' cost itemization. It was found, however, that when the 850 items were grouped into systems (mechanical, electrical, structural, etc.) there was a remarkably good correlation; within four or five per cent for similar buildings at a given location.

This correlation is significant as a measure of the practicality of computerization of the estimating process. It is also a useful tool for owners, designers and construction managers to apply in the budgeting process and in the evaluation of architectural options. That is, it reinforces confidence in the accuracy of systems estimates so that alternates can be reasonably appraised.

8 | PARTICIPATING OPTIONS OF SMALL PROFESSIONAL FIRMS

With few exceptions, most of what has gone before has dealt with the massive detail and demanding urgencies of time, cost and quality control on large projects. Implications of a big staff, technical and clerical, to handle these matters have been inevitable. The recurrent theme of "common sense," "no new professions" and "consultation for full service" may have been overwhelmed by the citations of large works. It may be useful, therefore, to reiterate some of those points that might contribute to the perspective for a small professional firm.

First, it should be borne in mind, and has been stated here and elsewhere, there never has been—and never will be—a truly professional architectural and engineering commission in which there was no "construction management." Conventional modes of practice have always called for procedures for getting the building designed and put in place. These procedures have been part of the stock in trade of the design professions and have been paid for by conventional fee structures. They have had the backup in the past of the delivery expertise of the contracting sector of the industry. The contractors have indeed performed many, but by no means all, of those services that now bear the label of "construction management" for which they have been paid through profit on the work.

No small professional firm should view the designation "construction management" with any alarm. As we have stated elsewhere, there is no "new profession." The practice of construction management (at whatever scale is appropriate to the scope of the small firm or its capacities to employ skills through consultation) is truly and only an extension of the professions with which they are already familiar.

Second, a professional firm of any size should realize that at some critical project size the task of management, under today's conditions of urgency and changing method, grows beyond the scope of conventional fee structures and beyond the capabilities of the in-house personnel of the small professional firm. That is the reason this work has attempted to identify and separate the elements of those services for which separate charges and special talents can be applied. In pursuit of that identification, the full roster of services that can be encountered in larger works has been used as a checklist. The implication is by no means that the full roster applies to every job or that only large jobs require construction management.

Third, the exact point at which either the job size or the professional firm size becomes critical is only that point at which the management services become separable as an identity and charge against the professional commission. Obviously, it is a moveable point, the location of which on an absolute scale depends entirely on the circumstances surrounding the project.

Fourth, in the gray zone above and below the critical size, architectural and engineering firms large or small will call on their own resources and preferences to decide whether and how to provide those services. A critical size of $5 million has been mentioned as a criterion of GSA and other public construction agencies. There is nothing sacred or profound about that figure. It represents a result of study and experience related to the particular operating histories of those agencies. Many small professional firms may find opportunities to proffer separate services professionally well below that figure. On the other hand, many small firms may find opportunities to accept commissions well above that figure in consideration of identifiable categories of additional management tasks for which they can equip themselves by either consultation or added staff.

One small firm of 8 to 10 people has reported that it recently took on the design and phased-construction delivery of a $7.5-million manufacturing facility. The client is one of long-standing with this firm, and the conditions of complexity, other than the 500,000 sq. ft. size, were not severe. An experienced field representative and assistant, paid directly by the client, were added to the operating staff. Otherwise, the firm operated through a normal AE contract. Any additional fee for the management of the project under accelerated procedures became a matter of negotiation after the fact. Admittedly, this is not an arrangement open to every practitioner, but it does demonstrate the extent of confidence that a long-standing client can develop toward a professional firm.

A fifth point to be considered by firms of any size contemplating the emergence of construction management as a separate professional service is the fact that both the client universe and the professional universe are increasingly aware of and sophisticated about the services involved. While small firms need have no fears, they should, for that very reason, be prepared to participate in this professional service wherever that is appropriate. The service is needed at the professional level today. It will be provided at whatever scale is required.

INDEX

Abbott, James F., 59
AGC, 69
Agency, 3, 4, 9, 12
AIA documents, 86
Amis Construction Services, 74, 112, 118
Anderson, Beckwith and Haible, 52
Architect-client relations, 2, 31, 61
Architect-Engineer, role of the, 7, 9, 20, 31, 61
Architect-Engineer, the small firm, 2, 42, 65, 121
Architects for U. Mass/Boston, 52

Banks, Richard, 71
Belluschi, Pietro, 52
Bolt, Baranek and Newman, 52
Bonding, 11, 49

California, University of, 58
Cambridge Seven Associates, 52
Canadian Imperial Bank of Commerce, 49
Caudill Rowlett Scott, 11, 92
Chisvin, Jack, & Associates, 50
Client, role of the, 2, 17, 60, 89
CM Associates, 92
Commerce Court, Toronto, 49
Computers in CM, 85, 103
    cost control with, 119
    cost of, 105
Construction consultant (definition), 4, 6, 9

Construction manager (definition), 4, 6, 9, 61
    skills required by, 26
Construction, phased, 3, 11, 13, 17
    (see also: Fast track)
Contingency reserves, 22, 41
Contract, the prototype, 83
Contractor as professional, 5, 25, 61, 70, 78
Contractors, general, 5, 12, 25, 61, 69, 74
Contracts and proposals, 79
Contracts, multiple,
    (see multiple contracts)
Cory, G. L., Company, 59
Cost control, 39, 119
Cost of computers, 105
Critical path method, 26, 38, 47
Critical size, 12

Decision, Design and Delivery, 4, 17
Definitions
    construction administrator, 4, 6, 9
    construction consultant, 4, 6, 9
    construction manager, 4, 6, 9
    management, 8
    project administrator, 4, 6, 9
    project manager, 4, 6, 9
Developer as client, 74
Documents,
    construction, 17
    drawn bid, 45
    standard, 86

INDEX

Edwards and Kelsey, 52
Estimating, conceptual, 40
Estimating, computerized, 119

Fast track, 3, 11
Fees, 11, 13, 19, 21, 76, 83
Fischer, Robert E., 49

General conditions on site, 28, 83, 96
General Services Administration, 15, 46, 60, 74, 83
Geometrics, Inc., 52
Golemon, Harry; Golemon and Rolfe, 43
Goody, Marvin E., and Clancy, John M., 52
Granek, G., & Associates, 50
Greenleaf Engineers, 52
Gregg, William J., 46
Guaranteed max, 43, 78
Guaranteed outside price (U. Cal.), 58

Haldeman and Goransson Associates, 52
Haley and Aldrich, 52
Hastings, Robert F., 4, 57

Insurance, 82

Kantz, R. Clayton, 59
Kunzig, Robert L., 46

Lammers, James I., 35
Le Messurier Associates, 52
Liability, 2, 20, 30, 42, 81, 102
Lincoln Hospital, 71

Main, Charles T., Inc., 52
Management system, computerized, 106
    reports, 110
Mason-Kiewit, 50
Massachusetts, University of, 52
Meathe, Philip J., Jr., 35
McKee, Gerald, Jr.; McKee-Berger-Mansueto, 17, 52, 101
Montoya, Fred, 72
Multiple contracts, 10, 12, 40, 69

Nash, Ralph C., Jr., 46
New York Authority, Port of, 47
New York State
    Facilities Development Corp., formerly Health and Mental Hygiene Facilities Improvement Corporation, 15, 65, 68
    University Construction Fund, 11, 32, 40, 65

O'Brien, Frank, 53
Organization for CM, 25, 66
    Charts, 34, 51, 55
Owner's responsibility, 16, 37, 57

Page & Steele, 49
Pei, I. M., 49
Perkins, Bradford, 53, 57, 101
Phased construction, 3, 11, 13, 16, 38, 71, 75
Port of New York Authority, 47
Professional relationships, 32
Professionalism, 1, 10
Project administrator (definition), 4, 6, 9
    services of, 31, 53, 61
Project anatomy, 36
Project coordinator (NYSUCF), 67
Project manager (definition), 4, 6, 9, 61
Public Buildings Service, GSA, 46, 60

Quantity survey, 74

Read, Philip G., 46
Reed, Campbell, 69
Roth, Emery, and Sons, 47

Safety, 89
Sasaki, Dawson, DeMay Associates, 52
Sayers & Associates, 50
Schickele, Hans G. R., 59
Services of CM, 27, 61, 87, 92
Size of project, critical, 12
Small firm participation, 2, 42, 65, 106, 121
Smith, Hinchman & Grylls, 11, 35, 40
Staffing, 81
Stephens, Donald J., 23
Stony Brook, 39
Subcontracting of CM services, 81
Subcontractors as source, 11, 14, 26, 78

Team, 3, 42, 52
Thomsen, Charles, 92
Tishman Company, 47, 75
Turner Construction Company, 35, 71

Urbahn, Max O., 71, 74
URBS, 59
UTAP, 3, 42

Weese, Harry, & Associates, 52
World Trade Center, 47

Yamasaki, Minoru, 47